THE CREDIT HANDBOOK

CHANGE YOUR CREDIT CHANGE YOUR LIFE

ERIC LAWRENCE FRAZIER MBA

ACKNOWLEDGMENTS

First, I would like to thank God for the inspiration He provides me to write. I love the love of God, and I am humbled to be saved by His grace and mercy.

This book is dedicated to everyone seeking to achieve the American Dream of homeownership (U.S. Department of Housing and Urban Development, 2025)[55]. Your credit, income, and debt management will help make your dream a reality (Fair Isaac Corporation, 2025)[14]. Pray about what you must do, and take action daily until God answers your prayers.

To my beautiful wife, Ruby Frazier, of 43 years—I love you more than words can say. You have been my rock and my greatest cheerleader since the day we met. Not a day goes by that I am not grateful for all you have done and continue to do for our family and me. I cannot imagine life without you. You make our house a home and give my life purpose and meaning.

To my four wonderful daughters—Jessica, Briana, Erica, and Raela —each of you holds a special place in my heart. You are a powerful, beautiful, and brilliant woman doing great things in real estate and in life. I am so proud of all of you.

To my grandchildren—Carrah, Chloe, Cameron, Ava, and Kobie—I love you very much and look forward to seeing the impact you will have on the world. To my sons-in-law, Virgil and Ohene "Bo," you are leaders, role models, and men of God. You show courage, love your families deeply, and inspire others through your example. I am thankful for the love and stability you bring into our family, and I am proud to be your father-in-law.

To my entire family—you inspire me with your unique lives and the great things you are accomplishing. Continue to buy real estate, build wealth, and pursue excellence. You make me proud to be the patriarch of our family.

Thank you to Kim Collier, Director of The Power Is Now Publishing. Your daily support, reminders, and expertise in publishing have been invaluable. What began as a vision has now grown into several published books.

Thank you to Goldy Ponce, Graphic Designer of The Power Is Now Graphic Design team. Your eye for design and ability to bring my vision to life are truly incredible.

Thank you to Daniel George and Alvin Magua, Managing Editors of The Power Is Now Magazine, for your research and assistance with this book.

Finally, thank you to our marketing team—you are fantastic! This book, along with the many others to come, will receive the attention it deserves because of your dedication, creativity, and professionalism. I sincerely appreciate your work.

And to you—the reader holding this book—thank you. I hope you enjoy it, learn from it, and share it with future homeowners (Consumer Financial Protection Bureau, 2023)[7]. Please give them the information you may not have received when you began working toward your dream of homeownership (U.S. Department of Housing and Urban Development, 2025)[55]. I know they will appreciate it.

THE CREDIT HANDBOOK

"Change your credit change your life"

978-1949722147 Print)

DISCLAIMER

The Credit Handbook is intended to help others on their way to better credit. The information presented is for informational purposes only and is solely the expression of the author's opinion. While every attempt has been made to verify any information presented in this book, the author is not responsible for any errors, inaccuracies, or omissions.

BUSINESS BOOKS

ERIC LAWRENCE FRAZIER, MBA BUSINESS BOOKS

POETRY COLLECTION

ERIC LAWRENCE FRAZIER, MBA POETRY BOOKS

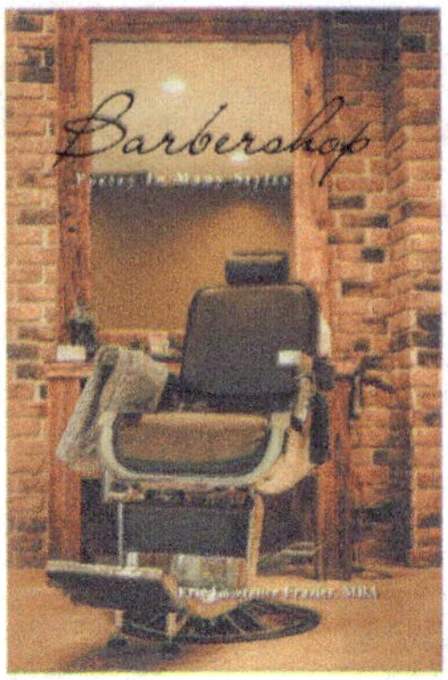

INTRODUCTION

Imagine leaving home at nineteen years of age, young and naïve, and going to school. You have no credit or understanding of credit or debt management, and you have had no real responsibility before leaving home. Now add taking on the responsibility of a wife and a home, and dropping out of college to work full time to make more money.

You can imagine the complete shock I encountered. Suddenly, I was sitting at the grown folks' table. It was time to contribute instead of being served.

I wanted to be on my own and I wanted to start my life, but looking back, I didn't have a clear understanding of what that meant. I didn't have a clue about establishing credit, budgeting my money, managing my expenses and debt, or all the responsibilities that come with maintaining a household and keeping a job. I also didn't have the legacy of knowledge that comes from parents who were financially savvy.

My mother was a stay-at-home mom and my dad worked at 7-Up Bottling Company and was a part-time minister. He knew the Bible and made sure I understood Biblical principles, but he didn't know anything about money or even how to succeed in the workplace. Nor was he the best example as a father, husband, provider, or businessman. I didn't have support, knowledge, the experience and or mentors to help me along the way. Financial literacy wasn't taught in my school, or the church.

By getting started so young in adult life and married life without that support, I didn't realize that I had enrolled myself in the School of Hard Knocks and would eventually graduate Summa Cum Laude with a PhD in credit, real estate, money management, marriage, and family. I learn the hard way and through trial and error and many mistakes, I have lost millions and made millions.

I am thankful that I am still ahead and that my gains have exceeded my losses, and that my knowledge and wisdom has grown exponentially. I am in a position today to help keep others from making the same mistakes I made, and to help them succeed in life. This is the reason why I am writing this book.

After forty years of marriage, four daughters with college degrees, millions of dollars in real estate both acquired and lost, millions in earnings, a degree in business and management and a master's degree in business and finance, billions in funded home loans over a forty year career of managing and originating home mortgages for major banks, and thousands of customers assisted in becoming homeowners, I'm an expert and equipped to help people learn real estate, loans, credit, business, and marriage.

I am an expert because of the sheer number of years I've been in practice as a husband, father, manager, and originator, working in financial services, real estate, credit, and education while raising a family.

I am dedicated to helping people achieve the American dream of homeownership, and to making a difference in the lives of people that will impact them for the rest of their lives. I know what homeownership did for me, and I also know how important credit is if you want to have any chance of building wealth and achieving your personal and financial goals in life. You must have good credit and a plan to obtain it if you are going to succeed.

Your experience may not be my experience. I was not born with a silver spoon in my mouth. I was born in a very humble environment, the oldest of seven kids living in San Bernardino, California, which was at the time the murder capital of the world. My parents did not have a formal education, but they did the very best they could to provide, protect and educate seven children.

If you are looking for a solid resource to build great credit that will lead to building wealth through buying a home—or multiple homes—then this book is for you. This book is not for anyone looking for a "quick credit fix." Rome wasn't built in a day, and your credit will not improve overnight. But with hard effort applied in the right direction, you will be on your way to financial success. Let's get started.

CHAPTER 1
YOUR CREDIT REPORT

"The secret of getting ahead is getting started."
— Mark Twain

A credit report is one of the most critical documents in your financial life. It is the collection of your debt and credit account information and how you handle them (Consumer Financial Protection Bureau, 2023)[7]. In addition, a credit report includes information about how you pay your bills, how much debt you've accumulated, where you work, and where you live. It also includes whether you have had a judgment (lawsuit) entered against you or filed for bankruptcy and whether you have had a vehicle repossessed or a home foreclosed (Federal Trade Commission, 2023)[45].

How Information Gets on a Credit Report

Credit reports are generally maintained by businesses known as credit reporting agencies or credit bureaus (Consumer Financial Protection Bureau, 2023)[7]. In the U.S., there are three major credit bureaus:

- TransUnion (TransUnion, 2025)[25]

- Experian (Experian, 2025)[44]
- Equifax (Consumer Financial Protection Bureau, 2023)[21]

Businesses and credit card companies send your financial information and payment history to these credit bureaus (sometimes all three, but at least one), who then report this information in your credit report (Government Accountability Office, 2022)[10]. Most of your loan accounts and credit card information are updated monthly on your credit report (Federal Reserve Bank of New York, 2023)[9]. However, some companies do not update credit reports with monthly payments; they only notify credit agencies when you fall behind on payments (Consumer Financial Protection Bureau, 2023)[7].

For instance, your cable bill is not automatically included in a credit report. But if you are more than six months behind on the payment, the account will be listed on the credit report as a collection (Consumer Financial Protection Bureau, 2023)[7]. Unfortunately, much of the information reported by credit card companies and businesses may be incorrect, so you must know what's on your credit report (Federal Trade Commission, 2023)[45].

How Information is Incorporated into a Credit Report

Credit reports incorporate basic and standard identifying information, including your full name, place of employment, and address (Consumer Financial Protection Bureau, 2023)[7]. Your credit report may also include previous addresses, misspellings of your name, and your current and previous employers.

A credit report is a comprehensive record of your financial life. It includes detailed information about your loans, credit cards, and public financial records (Federal Reserve, 2024)[1]. It covers all your credit card details, including credit limits, balances, usage, account status, account types, and payment history (Fair Isaac Corporation, 2025)[14]. It provides the loan amount, balances, and payment history for loans (Federal Reserve Bank of New York, 2023)[9]. It also lists public records such as foreclosure, bankruptcy, tax liens, and repossessions in separate sections (Consumer Financial Protection Bureau, 2023)[7].

Your credit report includes a list of companies that have checked your credit history due to a promotional screening or a credit application you submitted (Consumer Financial Protection Bureau, 2023)[7]. These credit checks are generally known as "inquiries." Your credit report will show inquiries from each party that has pulled your credit report, including companies that look at the information for promotional purposes (Consumer Financial Protection Bureau, 2023)[7]. A lender version of your credit report shows the detailed inquiries you asked when you put in any application (Consumer Financial Protection Bureau, 2023)[7].

Checking Your Credit Report

You need to order your credit report every year to ensure the details listed on the information are correct (Annual Credit Report, 2025)[51]. If you notice you have been a victim of identity theft, you should monitor your credit report more regularly (MyFICO Identity Theft Education, 2025)[41]. You should also check your credit report more often if you plan to apply for a significant loan or are seriously trying to repair your credit (Bankrate, 2025)[27]. You may order the credit report for free through a promotional offer, through a site set up by the government, by requesting one if your credit has been denied, or by purchasing a credit report from one of the three credit bureaus (Consumer Financial Protection Bureau, 2023)[7].

How to Read Your Credit Report

The credit reports from the three major credit bureaus will show how negative information can affect your credit (Federal Trade Commission, 2023)[45]. It will show why you have been turned down for your credit and whether someone tried to apply fraudulently for credit or a loan under your name (Consumer Financial Protection Bureau, 2023)[7]. Credit reports are especially crucial for you because lenders and credit card issuers review them to determine what interest rate they will offer you, whether you are a credit risk and the amount of your credit limit (Fair Isaac Corporation, 2025)[14].

Your credit reports may also be reviewed when purchasing insurance or renting an apartment (Consumer Financial Protection Bureau, 2023)[7]. Your credit score is used to summarize your credit report and creditworthiness (Fair Isaac Corporation, 2025)[14]. You will find it at the top of your report, ranging from 300 at the lowest to 850 at the highest (MyFICO, 2025)[26].

With so much information included in the report and its impact on your financial success, where should you even start when it comes to reviewing your credit reports?

Credit Reports are Generally Divided into 7 Sections

1. **Personal information.** Identity information on the credit reports can include;

- Name
- Birth date
- Social Security number
- Address
- Phone number
- Employer history

(Consumer Financial Protection Bureau, 2023)[7]. Your employment history may be included in the personal information section. You can add missing employer information or file a dispute to change incorrect information, which is usually unnecessary. The employer information listed on the credit reports is generally there to help cross-check your identity (Consumer Financial Protection Bureau, 2023)[7].

2. **Credit accounts or trade lines.** Your credit accounts are the bulk of your credit report and are dedicated to your history of managing your credit (Consumer Financial Protection Bureau, 2023)[7].

3. **Account Information.** The location of detailed information on accounts, including;

- Open accounts (installment, mortgage, and revolving credit)
- The specific dates accounts were opened and closed
- Credit utilization
- Payment history
- Loan payment status
- Current balances or limits
- Names of creditors (Fair Isaac Corporation, 2025)[14].

"If you're paying your bills on time or in full each month, this section will reflect that the account was paid as agreed," says John Danaher, president of Consumer Interactive at TransUnion (TransUnion, 2025)[25].

Suppose you find incorrect or wrong identity information on your credit reports. In that case, you may file a dispute and notify the credit bureau to change it (Consumer Financial Protection Bureau, 2023)[7]. Then, inform the creditor that you've reported the information to the credit bureau and requested an update (Consumer Financial Protection Bureau, 2023)[7].

4. **Collections.** This section will reflect the delinquent payment status if a loan goes into collections (Consumer Financial Protection Bureau, 2023)[7]. All late payments will be included on your credit report for up to seven years from the missed-payment date before they are deleted or removed by the credit agencies or bureaus (Federal Trade Commission, 2023)[45].

The Consumer Financial Protection Bureau recommends checking for the following mistakes:

- Accounts belonging to another person with the same name
- Incorrect or wrong payment history
- Accounts created or applied for through actual

. . .

5. **Identity theft** (Consumer Financial Protection Bureau, 2023)[7]

- Reinsertion of data previously corrected
- Incorrect credit limit or balance information
- Consumer statements

This credit report section can contain any statements submitted to the credit bureau (Consumer Financial Protection Bureau, 2023)[7]. For instance, if you have disputed some information and the dispute investigation was not resolved, your consumer statement could state the information provided.

6. **Public Records.**

- Liens.
- Bankruptcies.
- Foreclosures.
- Civil suits and judgments may appear in this section (Federal Trade Commission, 2023)[45].

A credit report can also include information on delinquent child support provided by a local child support agency or state or verified by any federal, state, tax returns, or local government agency (Consumer Financial Protection Bureau, 2023)[7].

7. **Inquiries.** Hard inquiries can hurt your credit scores negatively (Consumer Financial Protection Bureau, 2023)[7]. However, there are other reasons for reading this section closely. Hard inquiries usually occur when a financial institution checks your credit report to see if someone applied for credit or a loan in your name (Consumer Financial Protection Bureau, 2023)[7]. If you do not recognize

the inquiry, it may signify identity theft. The credit bureaus will allow you to block any inquiries attempted without your permission (MyFICO Identity Theft Education, 2025)[41].

Understanding Credit Score Ranges

Knowing how to read your credit report can help you understand how to improve your credit score. However, checking your credit report regularly is essential to watch for fraud and identity theft.

FICO 8 and VantageScore 3.0 are the most-used credit scoring models, ranging from 300 to 850. All lenders and creditors set their standards or rules for what constitutes an "excellent," "good," "fair," or "bad" score. However, credit scores generally fall into the following ranges (MyFICO, 2025)[26]:

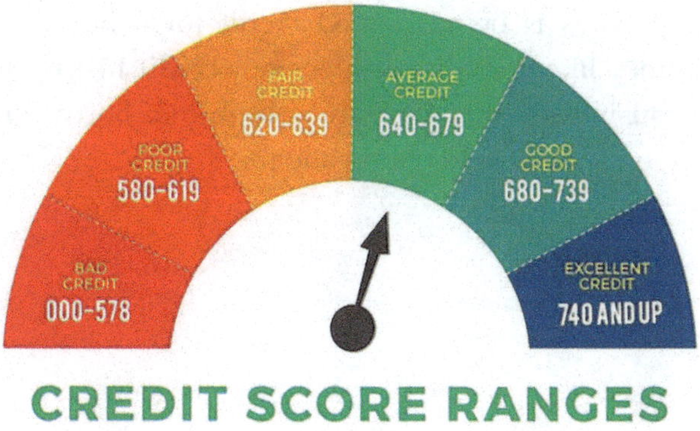

- 740 and up: Excellent credit
- 680-739: Good credit
- 640-679: Average credit,
- 620-639: Fair credit
- 580-619: Poor credit
- 300-578: Bad credit

VantageScore comprises the three major credit bureaus: Trans-

Union, Experian, and Equifax. The information used to establish both FICO and VantageScore scores is collected from the credit bureaus and is a factor in measuring risk and creating your score (Fair Isaac Corporation, 2025)[14].

How Does a Credit Score Impact Your Life?

A good credit score is vital for any person or family to have. Loans are a necessity in our world today. Quality of life is built on a solid credit history while maintaining a healthy credit score. All this must be considered when you think about applying for a loan or even a prepaid credit card.

Why It All Matters

A low credit score can seriously impact your life in many ways. One of the significant ways is being denied credit for a home purchase or something minor like a credit card. A poor credit history indicates to lenders and businesses that you are a high-risk borrower, and they should deny you if you try to obtain a loan.

Poor credit can also impact one's ability to obtain employment and cause one to pay more for utilities and car insurance.

When it comes to buying a home, a person with a lower credit score will have a higher interest rate. For example, a person with a FICO score 620 would pay 185 thousand dollars more on a five hundred-thousand-dollar, thirty-year fixed-rate mortgage than someone with the same mortgage with a FICO score of over 757 (Federal Reserve Bank of New York, 2023)[9].

A person with a score above 750 will also have a range of borrowing options, such as the capability to qualify for zero-interest credit cards, zero-interest financing on cars, and a very low-interest rate on a home mortgage.

A credit score affects much more than loan approvals. Here's a visual breakdown of how your score impacts your financial life:

Good credit gives you access to:

- Lower interest rates on mortgages and auto loans
- Easier approvals for rental housing
- Credit card rewards and low-interest offers
- Greater job opportunities
- Better insurance premiums
- Business loan qualification

Bad credit, on the other hand, leads to:

- Higher monthly payments
- Limited housing and job prospects
- Denials or high fees for credit
- Fewer borrowing options
- More stress and fewer financial choices

Creditors look at more than just credit scores

When you qualify for a mortgage or personal loan, a good credit score doesn't guarantee a lower interest rate – or even a loan approval. Creditors can gauge whether you will repay the money by looking at your credit score, debt load, and credit history. If you have a lot of debt but are paying your bills on time, you may have a good credit score.

What is (DTI) Debt-To-Income Ratio?

Your (DTI) debt-to-income ratio is the total monthly creditor payments reported on your credit report divided by your gross income and has proven to be a good determinant of whether you can repay a loan (Bankrate, 2025)[27].

Your debt-to-income ratio indicates whether you have the ability to pay, and it carries significant weight in lending decisions.

Other monthly obligations not on the credit report could be added to your debt-to-income ratio, like child support, alimony, state and federal income taxes, student loans, and judgments. These factors could increase your DTI and negatively impact your credit score.

How Much You Pay and Where You Live

Before you buy a home, all lenders will assess credit, income, and assets to mitigate the risk of default on the mortgage. If your credit score is low, the lender will consider your loan request as high risk and deny the loan. If you are approved for a mortgage loan, your credit score will determine the rate of interest you will pay. Your interest rate and term will directly affect the affordability of your monthly mortgage payment.

Never think that your credit is not important because you are not looking to buy a home right now. Having a credit score that is between good and great is imperative. If you rent, landlords review your credit to decide whether they will rent to you. They consider your lease as the bank makes your loan request. If you do not have good to excellent credit, your application to rent may be rejected (Fair Isaac Corporation, 2025)[14].

If you don't have cash to purchase a car, you must obtain a car loan. Your credit score not only determines whether you are eligible for the loan but also determines the interest rate and amount of the loan.

My recommendation is not to finance a car at all. If you can drive a vehicle your parents or relatives own that is not being used, it will be your best financial solution. That is the ideal solution if you can save money to pay cash for a car. But if you must finance a vehicle, you must have good or even excellent credit because a car payment will a#ect your ability to buy a home, depending on your income.

The higher your credit score, the better your terms will be.

Buying a $40,000 car with a low credit score will result in paying an interest rate in the 12 to 20 percent range. A five-year car loan will pay almost twice as much for the car. You will lose 30% of the value as soon as you drive it off the lot, And it will be worth 25% of the price you paid for it when you finally pay it off. If your interest rate is very high, you may need to extend the term to seven or even ten years to have an affordable payment, which makes *the ultimate cost of the car even more expensive. Having a low credit score means you pay more.*

It is my recommendation, regardless of your credit score, to pay cash. Buy a used car or borrow a friend or relative's car that is not being used until you can save and purchase a car in cash.

Low credit scores limit your options, and only a few creditors will give you a loan. These creditors are actually predators, taking advantage of your low credit score status to charge you a higher interest rate and absorb its fees to compensate for the higher risk you demonstrate in defaulting on the loan.

You have one thing providing them a reason to extend the credit: the ability to pay. You demonstrate the ability to pay them, perhaps no one else, because you will pay more in interest on payments on credit cards, car loans, home loans, and anything else you finance.

You will pay more because of a low credit score, adversely affecting your ability to save money and become debt-free.

Many employers and companies conduct credit checks as a part of their hiring process. They check credit reports and credit scores. If you cannot demonstrate your financial responsibility, an employer might be reluctant to hire you. Some employers or companies check your credit scores before giving a raise or promotion, especially for executive or financial-related positions.

The majority of new businesses or startups need to borrow money. As a result, you may need to obtain a small business loan. Among all the other things, you should have a good credit score to qualify for a business loan.

5 Immediate Action Steps to get started today

1. **Pull All 3 Credit Reports (Not Just One)**
2. Go to AnnualCreditReport.com and download your reports from **Experian, Equifax, and TransUnion**. These reports are free once a week, and each may have different info (Annual Credit Report, 2025)[51].

Why it matters: You can't fix what you haven't seen. Lenders check all 3.

3. **Highlight Every Negative or Suspicious Item**

Print your reports (or save digitally), and **highlight anything** that looks off:

- Collections
- Late payments
- Accounts you don't recognize
- Multiple hard inquiries

Think of this like marking the leaks before repairing a roof.

The Bottom Line

Your credit report is more than a file—it's a financial fingerprint. It's a snapshot of your financial character and responsibility. Lenders, employers, insurers, and landlords all review it to assess your reliability.

By checking it regularly and knowing how to read and interpret it, you're not just protecting your score, you're protecting your future.

In the next chapter, we'll dig into **what affects your credit score and how to take control of it**, starting today.

CHAPTER 2
LEARNING ABOUT FICO

"If you work hard at something, great things will happen." Neal McDonough

The most popular credit concept is the FICO score. A FICO score is the rating that a person gets that helps banks, creditors, and other financial institutions assess the risk they are taking if they decide to lend money to that individual (Fair Isaac Corporation, 2025)[14]. When a person is applying for a loan, taking out a mortgage, or even just obtaining a credit card, the FICO score is the most reliable number for financial institutions to assess the level of risk they would be taking on (Federal Reserve Bank of New York, 2023)[9].

This isn't just theory. I've lived it—as a borrower, a banker, a husband, a father, and an advocate. Now, I'm sharing it with you.

What Is a FICO Score?

FICO stands for Fair Isaac Corporation (Fair Isaac Corporation, 2025)[14]. The organization was established in 1956 and released the first total FICO score in 1989 (Fair Isaac Corporation, 2025)[14]. As a pioneer in introducing the first credit risk score in the world, the organization's reputation has grown into the big name that it is today (Securities and Exchange Commission, 2023)[12].

Your FICO score is a three-digit number between 300 and 850 (MyFICO, 2025)[26]. Higher scores signal lower credit risk. Lenders use it to decide:

- Whether to lend you money
- What interest rate to offer
- What terms you qualify for
- Whether to approve your application at all

In the credit industry, if a person's FICO score is high, they will likely get approved with competitive rates and terms (Fair Isaac Corporation, 2025)[14]. If their FICO score is low, they may receive disadvantageous rates and terms.

"FICO is what decides if you get approved. Everything else is just a preview."

In addition to the "classic" FICO score, there are industry-specific models (Fair Isaac Corporation, 2025)[14]:

- **FICO Auto Score:** puts more weight on past auto loan performance.
- **FICO Mortgage Scores:** older versions (FICO 2, 4, and 5) required by Fannie Mae and Freddie Mac.
- **FICO 10 and 10T:** newer models that incorporate "trended data" — your patterns of borrowing and repayment over time.

The following are the **FICO SCORE ranges** and precisely what they mean (MyFICO, 2025)[26]:

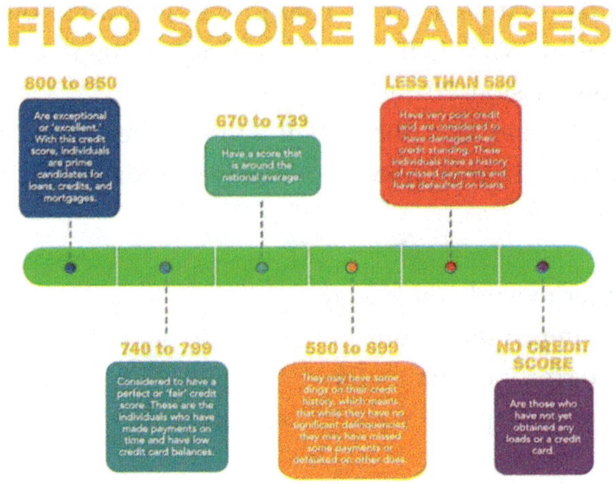

- **800 to 850:** FICO scores ranging from 800 to 850 are exceptional or "excellent." With this credit score, individuals are prime candidates for loans. They get the lowest interest rates on their loans, credits, and mortgages. These are people with a strong credit history and no late payments. They do not pay just the minimum on their credit cards and know how to handle every credit card and loan payment on time.

- **740 to 799:** Individuals with a score between 740 and 799 are considered to have a perfect or "fair" credit score. These individuals have made payments on time and have low credit card balances.

- **670 and 739:** People with a credit score between 670 and 739 have a score around the national average (the national FICO score average is 695) (Federal Reserve Bank of New York, 2023)[9]. Those under this category generally receive slightly higher but still competitive interest rates. Unfortunately, those under this credit score range may have difficulty obtaining certain types of credit.

- **580 to 669:** If a person's credit score is 580 to 669, they may have some dings on their credit history, which means that while they have no significant delinquencies, they may have missed some payments or defaulted on other dues. Lenders may still extend credit to those in this category, but they will not receive competitive rates compared to those with a superior credit score.

- **Less than 580:** Those with a FICO score of less than 580 have very poor credit and are considered to have damaged their credit standing. These individuals have a history of missed payments, have defaulted on a loan, have judgments against them, have collection accounts, or have declared bankruptcy (Consumer Financial Protection Bureau, 2023)[7].

- **No Score:** Those with no credit score have yet to obtain any loans or credit cards.

Anyone can achieve a perfect credit score of 850 (Fair Isaac Corporation, 2025)[14]. However, one should not lose hope if they do not have an ideal credit score. Generally, those with a score of 800 or above have high incomes, limited debt, low credit card utilization, and very high credit limits. It takes the correct type of credit, time to get to that level, and a perfect payment history to stay there (MyFICO, 2025)[26].

Why Lenders Use FICO

Lenders use FICO because (Fair Isaac Corporation, 2025)[14]:

- It's **predictive** of risk — who will repay vs. default.
- It's **standardized** across all borrowers.
- It's **regulator-approved** for most loan types.
- It gives **them** confidence in making loan decisions.

Here are the top ten strategies to obtain and maintain a high FICO score:

1. Obtain and maintain at most five to eight lines of credit (MyFICO, 2025)[26]. If possible, have one mortgage, car loan, two to three credit cards, student loan, installment loan, and personal loan.

2. Never confuse available credit for income. Credit is not income. It is a convenient way to access cash.

3. Pay off credit card balances at the end of the month, and never carry a balance for more than thirty days (Consumer Financial Protection Bureau, 2023)[7].

4. Only obtain an installment loan for up to twenty-four months. Keep all car loans between twenty-four and thirty-six months. If you need more than thirty-six months, you are buying too many cars.

5. Never miss a payment. Never charge over your credit limit. Never exceed the term of any installment loan (Fair Isaac Corporation, 2025)[14].

6. Never allow any credit card issue or dispute on any debt to go into collection (Consumer Financial Protection Bureau, 2023)[7]. Pay it off. Do not put your credit in harm's way over a dispute. Pay the debt and deal with it later.

7. Never declare bankruptcy or go into foreclosure on a home loan (Federal Trade Commission, 2023)[45]. It may take years to recover.

8. Never co-sign on a loan for anyone unless it is your child, and even then, do not co-sign for your child if you know they are irresponsible and have demonstrated irresponsible behavior for as long as you have known them (Consumer Financial Protection Bureau, 2023)[7]. People do not change, even children.

9. Only close an account if there is an annual fee.

10. Only make large purchases on credit cards if you have the money to pay it off immediately.

You have the power to change your life and the power to improve your credit. A powerful correlation exists between having a great life and excellent credit. Great credit will lower your cost of credit when it is time to buy a home, finance a car, obtain a job, and other necessities in life (Fair Isaac Corporation, 2025)[14]. You can change your credit now, and it's up to you to make that happen.

Achieving your financial goals requires discipline, commitment, and consistency. The Power Is Now Media supports your journey to excellent credit. For more information and support on obtaining good credit, join our homebuyers seminars at The Power Is Now: https://thepowerisnow.com/membership/

Now that you know the range of FICO scores, it is essential to understand how your score gets calculated and how you can track it. What are the factors that affect your FICO score? What determines the three-digit score that could mean renting versus buying a home? This section aims to answer these questions and provide an in-depth analysis of how individuals can calculate and track their FICO score.

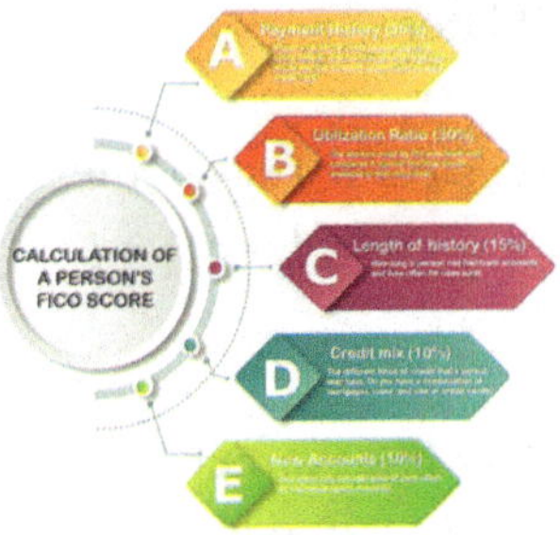

Calculation of your FICO Score

The FICO score is not just three digits. It is the mathematical indicator of an individual's spending and debt management behavior (Fair Isaac Corporation, 2025)[14]. It is the quantitative culmination of an individual's paying habits. The following are key factors in calculating a person's FICO score:

1. Payment History (35%) – This is the most important factor since it looks at how timely an individual pays for their debts (MyFICO, 2025)[26]. It records every missed payment, every default, and every single time you pay the minimum amount due on your credit card.

2. Utilization Ratio (30%) – This concept is a little more complicated than others since it looks at the amount owed by the individual and compares it to the total credit available to that individual (Fair Isaac Corporation, 2025)[14]. How much of the loan is being used? If an individual is close to maximizing the limit on his card, then it is likely that he might miss payments and default on his loan or credit card. This one is confusing because while the banks would want every cardholder to maximize their credit usage every month, they frown upon those who do so because of the increased likelihood that they will miss payments.

3. Length of history (15%) – This factor considers how long a person has had bank accounts and how often he uses them. The goal here is to look at the tendency of an individual to stay with the same bank or credit card provider. The more loyal a person is to the provider, the better it is for his credit score (MyFICO, 2025)[26].

4. Credit mix (10%) – The score considers the different kinds of credit a person may have (Fair Isaac Corporation, 2025)[14]. Does the credit consist of mortgages, loans, and credit cards? Or is an individual's debt history limited and focused primarily on credit cards? This behavior is considered, but it will take a while to positively or negatively impact a FICO score.

5. New accounts (10%)—This one asks how often an individual opens a new account (Fair Isaac Corporation, 2025)[14]. If one opens many new accounts at the same time, it will decrease their score. However, this factor plays a small role in the overall FICO score.

Tracking your FICO Score:

It is not hard to track your FICO score, and there are different services – both paid and free – with which to do so (MyFICO, 2025)[26]. The following are the best ways to track your FICO score:

Your credit card provider – An individual's credit card provider has a copy of his credit score. These providers allow the credit card holder to glimpse his credit score.

Credit score providers – Some service providers, such as Credit Concierge, Credit Sesame, and Fico.com, offer free information about a person's credit score (MyFICO, 2025)[26]. However, you must give your full name, address, and social security number to get the service, so regarding data privacy, it may not be a perfect option for everyone.

While the services vary and the ratings have different versions—which will be discussed in the next section—it is essential for individuals to take appropriate actions to keep their credit score at the right level. No matter how good an individual may be at tracking their credit score, if they do not follow the rules for keeping their credit score high, they will lower their score instead of increasing it.

The FICO score is more complex than you might expect. It has many different versions. Although the differences in the scores are not far from each other, it is still essential for an individual to know the various versions of the FICO score and what each score means (Fair Isaac Corporation, 2025)[14].

How many FICO scores are there?

According to FICO, there are more than 50 different versions of the credit score, and they are constantly being updated to give a more comprehensive picture of an individual's financial status (Fair Isaac Corporation, 2025)[14].

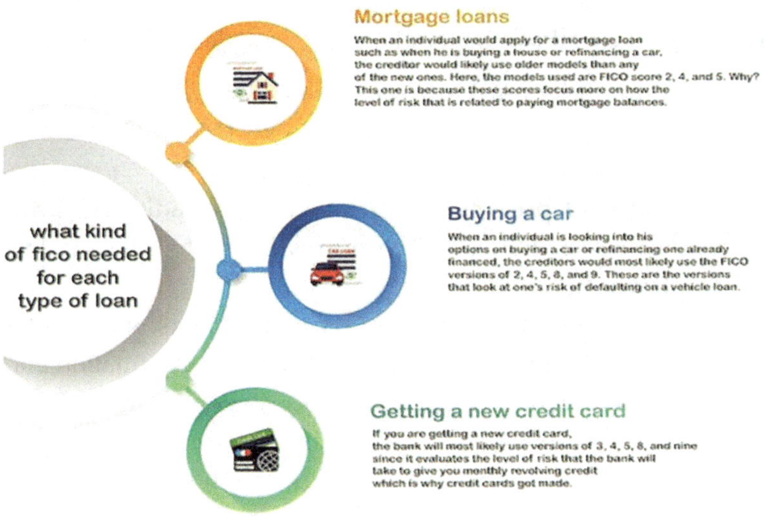

What Kind of FICO is Needed for each Type of Loan

Everyone should know how to keep their score healthy and what kind of FICO score the creditor will use. Each version of the FICO score uses a different algorithm to calculate the score (Fair Isaac Corporation, 2025)[14].

While FICO has released many new and improved versions, some creditors still use the older scoring models to apply for specific kinds of credit. Different industries use different kinds of credit scores because they also apply the scoring model to particular types of credit (Fair Isaac Corporation, 2025)[14]. For example:

Mortgage loans. When an individual is applying for a loan – such as buying a house or refinancing a car – the creditor will likely use FICO scores 2, 4, and 5 (Fair Isaac Corporation, 2025)[14]. These scores focus more on the risk level of paying off a mortgage.

Buying a car. When an individual considers his options for buying or refinancing a vehicle, creditors will most likely use FICO versions 2, 4, 5, 8, 9, 10, and 10T (Fair Isaac Corporation, 2025)[14]. These versions assess one's risk of defaulting on a vehicle loan.

Getting a new credit card. If you are getting a new credit card, the bank will use versions 3, 4, 5, 8, 9, 10, and 10T since they evaluate the level of risk that the bank will take to give you monthly revolving credit (Fair Isaac Corporation, 2025)[14].

Understanding what credit bureaus use is vital. Credit bureaus utilize various versions of the FICO score depending on the type of credit an individual is applying for (Consumer Financial Protection Bureau, 2023)[7]. Keeping track of these different versions can be challenging, but staying informed is essential. The newer versions often consider factors that the older versions do not, and it's up to the bureau's discretion to decide which models they want to use.

The most recent FICO score update.

FICO 10 and 10T. These new versions introduce additional factors and trend data to the FICO score 9. While FICO 9 considers common factors that could impact an individual's creditworthiness, such as medical bills, collections, and rent payments, FICO 10 and 10 T use the same guidelines but are more predictive (Fair Isaac Corporation, 2025)[14]. This section will delve into FICO 9 and the changes for FICO.

THE LATEST CREDIT SCORE: FICO 9, 10, and 10T

What is FICO 9?

Many credit bureaus began using FICO 9 at the beginning of 2016. It considers new factors that pose more risk to credit while reducing the effects of some factors with less impact, as shown by some studies (Fair Isaac Corporation, 2025)[14].

What factors are used to compute an individual's FICO 9 score?

These new factors, carefully selected to reflect the evolving credit landscape, are now part of the FICO 9 score calculation. Understanding these factors can help you navigate the credit world more effectively.

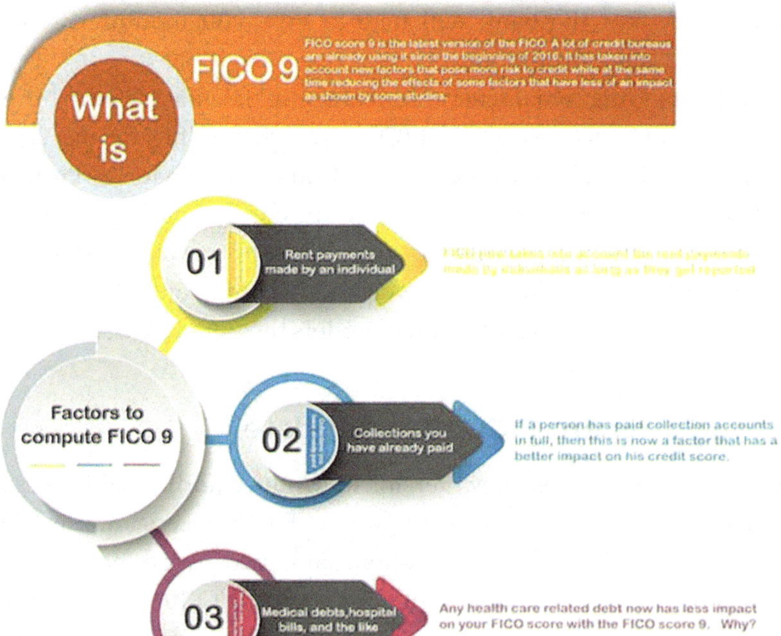

Factors to Compute FICO 9

Rent payments made by an individual. Score calculations are becoming more in-depth. FICO now considers rent payments made by individuals as long as they get reported (Fair Isaac Corporation, 2025)[14]. If you have defaulted on payment of your rent or have been missing rent payments, this is considered and computed with the algorithm to give creditors a more holistic view of your credit risk.

Collections you have already paid. If a person has paid collection accounts in full, this is now a factor that better impacts his credit score (Fair Isaac Corporation, 2025)[14]. However, if you have defaulted on paying your cable, water, or credit card bills that have already reached collection, you may need to look at how you will explain them since they are now taken into account by credit bureaus. On the upside, however, collections that have been paid off create a level of commitment from the individual that they do not want any unpaid debt.

Medical debts, hospital bills, etc. Any healthcare–related debt now has less of an impact on your FICO score with the FICO 9 (Fair Isaac Corporation, 2025)[14].

Some research indicates that unpaid medical accounts are less indicative of credit risk than payable non-medical accounts. While around forty-three million Americans have overdue medical debt, the risk involved is less critical than some think. With FICO Score 9, the factor looked at is whether or not the bills reach the level of collections. This different treatment is indicative of how FICO credit score calculations have evolved.

The FICO Score 9 algorithm stands out for its comprehensive approach to credit risk assessment. It considers a wide range of factors, offering a more complete view of an individual's credit risk compared to other credit scores (Fair Isaac Corporation, 2025)[14]. This detailed understanding can empower lenders and individuals to make informed decisions about lending and managing their credit.

How are FICO 10 and FICO 10T different?

In October 2020, FICO introduced the new FICO 10 and 10T scoring algorithms (Fair Isaac Corporation, 2025)[14]. This is the first time FICO has offered two versions of a general FICO score. The score that got consumer attention is the FICO 10T, which stands for trended data. Traditional FICO is a snapshot and follows the same reasoning as previous versions. In contrast, the 10T looks at your credit trends over the past 24 months and is more predictive (Fair Isaac Corporation, 2025)[14].

When will lenders start using FICO 10 & 10T?

FICO 10 scores are now available for the three major credit bureaus (Consumer Financial Protection Bureau, 2023)[7]. Most lenders still use FICO 8 for most non-mortgage lending decisions. FICO 2, 4, or 5 are used by mortgage lenders (Fair Isaac Corporation, 2025)[14]. In October 2022, the Federal Housing Finance Agency(FHFA) approved the use of FICO 10T by government-sponsored enterprises Fannie Mae and Freddie Mac (Federal Housing Finance Agency, 2022)[53].

How might FICO 10 and 10T affect your score?

When using the FICO 10 scoring models, your scores may drop if (Fair Isaac Corporation, 2025)[14]:

- You have applied for additional credit or consolidated credit card bills with a personal loan, and your balances are high again.
- You are living on credit cards, but your balances are growing, and you can't seem to pay them down.
- You have missed a payment. Under FICO 10, the penalty for 30 days past due is harsher than in previous models.

However, your score will most likely rise if you have been penalized for temporary high balances in the past. The 10T looks at balances over time and sees you paying down a temporary high balance (Fair Isaac Corporation, 2025)[14].

4 Steps to a Higher Score on the FICO 10 & 10T

1. Pay balances on credit cards (Fair Isaac Corporation, 2025)[14]. Consistently high statement balances — or rising balances — can suggest financial difficulty.
2. Avoid missing a payment (MyFICO, 2025)[26].
3. Start an emergency fund (Federal Reserve, 2024)[1]. Rising balances on credit cards could hurt your scores.
4. Avoid using credit cards again if you consolidate your debt with a personal loan (Fair Isaac Corporation, 2025)[14]. FICO 10T will penalize you for it.

FICO 10T and Trended Data

FICO 10T doesn't just look at your current balances—it looks at your behavior over the past 24 months (Fair Isaac Corporation, 2025)[14].

- If you carry a balance every month → penalty
- If you pay down balances → reward
- If you rack up debt after paying it off → penalty
- If you gradually reduce debt → reward

Summary - Key Lessons About FICO

- FICO is used in 90% of lending decisions (Fair Isaac Corporation, 2025)[14].
- FICO 2, 4, 5 are still used for mortgages (Fair Isaac Corporation, 2025)[14].
- FICO 10T tracks your 24-month behavior (Fair Isaac Corporation, 2025)[14].
- You need to know which version matters for your goal.
- Free scores ≠ loan scores (MyFICO, 2025)[26].

- Understanding the rules is how you win (Fair Isaac Corporation, 2025)[14].

CHAPTER 3
BUILDING GOOD CREDIT WHEN YOU HAVE NONE

"The secret of getting ahead is getting started." Mark Twain

For newcomers with no credit history, a lingering question may be how to get a credit score in the first place. Building credit can seem challenging, even tricky, at times. But following a few vital steps can bring you closer to building a great credit score—and a better life. Patience is key when it comes to earning a credit score. A credit account must be open for six months or more, as you will need at least one creditor to report your activity to the credit bureaus (myFICO, 2025)[26]. Remember, building credit is a journey, not a sprint.

There are several ways to create your first credit history, including a credit-builder loan, secured credit cards, a co-signed loan, or an authorized user status on another person's card (e.g., parent, spouse, or sibling) (Consumer Financial Protection Bureau, 2023)[7]. Whichever method you choose to earn your first credit score, be sure to use it in a way that would ultimately result in a good credit score.

Building great credit is relatively easy when you know how to do it. Below are six steps to building an excellent credit score and proving your creditworthiness to potential creditors.

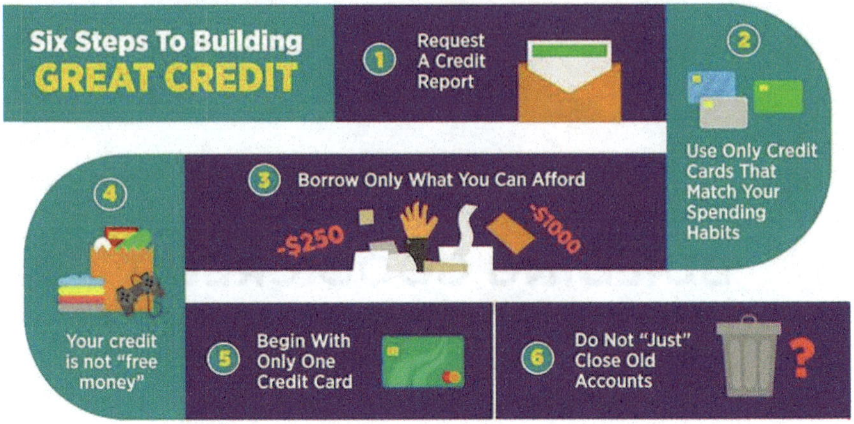

1. **Request a Credit Report**

You need to be informed to know where to start. So start with requesting your current credit report. Thanks to the Fair Credit Reporting Act, you are entitled to a yearly free credit report from the three major nationwide consumer credit bureaus—Experian, Equifax, and TransUnion (Federal Trade Commission, 2023)[45]. You can access the reports on Annual-CreditReport.com, a website run jointly by all three major consumer credit bureaus (Annual Credit Report, 2025)[51].

These agencies offer the same services, but the information on their respective credit reports may differ. Therefore, you must take the time to thoroughly inspect each report for errors and suspicious activities. If you discover a discrepancy, refer to the credit agency's website for information on how to fix it. Alternatively, you can contact them directly for help (Consumer Financial Protection Bureau, 2023)[7].

2. **Use Only Credit Cards That Match Your Spending Habits**

Understanding the payment terms and interest rates of a credit card is crucial in making a choice that aligns with your spending habits. This knowledge can potentially save you money in the long run. For instance, if you find it challenging to pay off your balance monthly, opting for a card with lower interest rates, even if it means sacrificing the rewards of higher-rate cards, could be a wise move (Bankrate, 2025)[27]. If you have a history of late payments, be cautious of cards with too-good-to-be-true offers. Good examples are some store cards promising zero interest. The monthly rates and annual fees for these can rise sharply and unexpectedly

3. **Borrow Only What You Can Afford**

If you're looking to purchase items you ordinarily cannot afford, then you probably should not be obtaining a credit card in the first place. Misuse of credit is the fastest way to run into debt and create credit trouble. Borrowing only what you need is the best way to avoid credit trouble (Consumer Financial Protection Bureau, 2023)[7].

4. **Do Not Treat Credit as "Free Money"**

Take control of your credit card usage by only charging what you can immediately pay off. Remember, credit is a tool for convenience, not a substitute for cash. By avoiding over-leveraging and using credit as income, you can establish a positive credit history. Prove to yourself and your creditors that you only borrow what you can pay back— and on time. This approach not only helps you avoid unnecessary debt but also instills a sense of financial empowerment. The same applies to loans. Borrow only the amount you can afford to pay despite what your creditor says you qualify for or the benefits you may get by opting for a higher amount. Also, when presented with "potentially" amazing loan offers and you feel tempted to "go all the way," remember that a creditor is in business for profit. No matter how "amazing" a loan may look, it's not for your benefit but for the benefit of your creditor. Don't get trapped! (Consumer Financial Protection Bureau, 2023)[7].

5. **Begin with Only One Credit Card**

Avoid opening too many cards too soon because you are human.

Most first-time credit card users accumulate too many cards initially and set themselves up for failure. With several credit cards to use, you will sooner than later become prone to overspending. With overspending comes debt and debt repayment difficulties. If you're considering obtaining more than two credit cards, it's important to weigh the benefits and risks. On one hand, they can be a useful resource in building your emergency fund. On the other hand, applying for multiple credit lines in a short period can have a negative impact on your credit score (Fair Isaac Corporation, 2025)[14]. It can reduce the average length of your credit lines and result in numerous hard inquiries on your credit report (Consumer Financial Protection Bureau, 2023)[7].

6. **Do Not "Just" Close Old Accounts**

Once you finally get a credit card and start building your credit, the key to building credit is not to close old accounts. The longer you have had a credit line open, the more helpful it is to your credit score. Let older credit accounts stay open; they are necessary to increase your average credit age and build good credit. If you must close old accounts, realize they will not be removed from your credit report immediately. It usually takes five to ten years for an account to be dropped entirely from your report by the credit bureaus (Federal Trade Commission, 2023)[45]. A stolen identity can be devastating financially for anyone. Records say that fifteen million Americans were victims of identity theft in 2016 alone (USA Today, 2017)[47]. Hackers can and will strike at any time. No one method can guarantee 100 percent protection from these thieves. But if precautionary steps are taken, you will be better prepared to secure your information against these fraudsters. They gain access to your personal information by stealing bills, financial statements, or discarded receipts—dumpster diving.

- They could potentially steal your wallet containing credit cards and card details.
- They fetch your information through spam calls or emails (Consumer Reports, 2025)[48].

- They can steal your information over open wireless networks with hacking apps / software (Consumer Reports, 2025)[48].

It is almost too easy for an identity thief to apply for a credit card or any other financial account in your name once they can get your social security number, date of birth, or any other personal informa tion through the above methods (Consumer Financial Protection Bureau, 2023)[7]. Identity theft is a silent predator, often going unnoticed until the collections calls start pouring in for credit card bills charged with our identities. By then, the damage may have been done, leaving us to deal with the aftermath.

4 Signs of a Stolen Identity:

1. Bank transactions or credit card purchases you don't recognize (Federal Trade Commission, 2023)[45]
2. Fresh credit inquiries or accounts you don't remember opening on your credit report (Annual Credit Report, 2025)[51]
3. Missing mail or mail from unknown billing agencies (Federal Trade Commission, 2023)[45]
4. Merchants are refusing your checks (Consumer Reports, 2025)[48]

So what can you do to protect your credit and save yourself from the heartache of identity theft?

1. Physically Secure Personal Information

It is always wise to stay security-conscious online. Keep vital documents like your social security card and birth certificates away from easy reach. While at it, ensure your physical documents are also inaccessible to identity thieves. Alert the Social Security Administration and the Internal Revenue Service if a thief gets hold of your social security number (Federal Trade Commission, 2023)[45].

Most financial service providers will require that you file a report and fill out an identity theft affidavit (MyFICO, 2025)[41]. Filing an affidavit is easy and takes only a few minutes. To file a police report, visit your nearest police station with your affidavit and explain the situation. Opt for paperless transactions in all your financial dealings. If, for some reason, you are unable to go entirely paperless, make good use of a shredder. Shredders eliminate the possibility of leaving behind trails that these scammers can use to exploit your credit (Federal Trade Commission,

2023)[45]. Avoid dumping credit reports or bank statements in your garbage. These are often targets for identity thieves. Use a shredder instead. Shred junk mail, too. Particularly pre-approved credit card offers.

2. Stay Vigilant While Shopping

Stay cautious when out shopping with your cards. Ensure you know where your purse/wallet is at all times. Don't be too trusting; a shop attendant can take pictures of your credit card without your knowledge. Also, avoid leaving your credit cards in a jacket or coat pocket, even for a few minutes. Please do not disclose your PIN to anyone, nor have it written down anywhere (TransUnion Article, 2025)[49].

3. Keep a Close Eye on Your Financial Statements

Thoroughly study all credit cards and bank statements, and pay attention to charges, no matter how small they may seem. Contact your credit card provider or bank to ascertain more details if you need to remember to make a particular charge. You should also know your due dates and place a call to inquire if you are still waiting to receive an expected bill. Study every insurance claim and ensure you have received the care you are paying for. Look out for suspicious activities with your taxes, as tax refunds are frequently easy targets for thieves. If you receive a tax notice from a job you have never held, file a report and demand an investigation. File taxes early to prevent the crooks from stealing your tax refund or identity with your social security number (Annual Credit Report, 2025)[51].

4. Freezing Your Credit

If you suspect irregularities in your financial records, the first line of action may be to freeze your credit to stop all credit activity immediately. This prevents fraudsters from generating new accounts in your name. You can request this service for free from the three major credit bureaus: Experian, Equifax, and TransUnion (Annual Credit Report, 2025)[51].

5. Don't Bare It All Online

You might love to share exciting moments in your life with friends and family on social media. Identity thieves, who also are online, are out to steal even the most minor personal details you share. Revealing sensitive information such as your mother's maiden name, your fourth-grade teacher's name, or your new pet's name may place you at a higher risk of getting scammed, even though it may seem harmless. Keep your personal life private. It's alright if you don't tell your online "buddies" what "Maxwell" your pet had last night or use captions like "my mom Emily Stuart has always looked like a "Model" on old photos of a parent (Stuart being your mother's maiden name). Additionally, do not click on suspicious links from anyone (Consumer Reports, 2025)[48].

6. Set Up Purchase Alerts

Nearly all banks and credit card companies provide the option of getting notifications that let you keep tabs on all activities in your account. If you sign up for these instant notifications, you will be alerted immediately when your credit is used to make a purchase. Signing up may also mean dealing with constant notifications from purchases you make. But that is a small sacrifice to pay to stay ahead of fraudsters. When purchases are charged to your account, you are notified; if you made the purchase, you can check if your merchant charged you right. If you didn't make the purchase, you can quickly shut down the card and request a new one. You may not be held accountable for all losses. Still, you can do your part by reporting after a single suspicious transaction rather than waiting to find and file disputes over several purchases on your monthly credit report (TransUnion Article, 2025)[49]. Some credit companies and banks have recently made it possible to lock and unlock credit cards through their mobile apps. This feature is easy to use. Can't find your card or have just been alerted to a transaction you know nothing about? Lock the card immediately! What if you later find it in your purse or remember using it as a bookmark a week ago? Reverse your action by unlocking. It's that simple!

7. Use Strong, Unique Passwords

We've all been advised against using predictable passwords for critical and sensitive accounts. While you may know that already, remember that personal details like your name, date of birth, and siblings' names are equally ill-advised as they can easily be predicted. Experts also recommend that you avoid using words found in the dictionary (TransUnion Article, 2025)[49].

Get creative with your passwords; craft elaborate ones with uppercase and lowercase letters, symbols, and numbers. Even better, have a password manager create, save, and automatically input complex passwords for you on different websites. Experts also recommend using a different password for every account. This way, if your password for an account is ever stolen, the crooks will not have access to your other accounts. I recommend Lastpass.com; It's a company I trust with and use for all my passwords.

8. Password-Protect Your Mobile Devices

If you do not use passwords, devices like your smartphones can pose real risks. Just like you update your PC, update all software and apps, and use difficult-to-guess passwords alongside two-factor authentication when available. Two-factor authentication services are available on nearly every device. Avoid public Wi-Fi, turn Bluetooth off when not in use, and avoid free apps when possible, as they can sometimes come loaded with malware. Your data can be monitored and stolen through them. Enter your passwords only on trusted and secure websites. Do not give in to unsolicited requests for financial details (Consumer Reports, 2025)[48].

Although our world may never be entirely rid of identity thieves, practical measures such as using strong passwords and checking your reports regularly are just as important as knowing how to respond if you ever fall prey to identity thieves. These thieves can target anybody, and that is something you have no control over. However, you can reduce your exposure and make it much more difficult for fraudsters to succeed.

The ever-advancing security technology does not deter them, but your measures can make you a formidable opponent. Staying ahead by closely monitoring your account activities is the best way to keep on the winning side of the unending war against identity theft.

Even with these methods in place, you'll have to review your credit reports regularly and accounts with sensitive information, and for a good reason. While it may be saddening to think about, the fact is that when scammers gain access to any of your personal information, they may have it forever and can go on committing fraudulent activities in your name. Always be aware.

POWER MOVES (ACTION STEPS YOU CAN TAKE)

Pull All Three Reports

Get free reports from Equifax, Experian, TransUnion via AnnualCreditReport.com at least annually (and before major applications) (Annual Credit Report, 2025)[51]. Scan for errors, duplicates, and identity-theft red flags (Consumer Financial Protection Bureau, 2023)[7].

Automate On-Time Payments

Put every recurring bill on auto-pay (at least the minimum for cards) (MyFICO, 2025)[26]. Use calendar reminders and bank alerts to avoid the single costliest mistake: a late payment (Fair Isaac Corporation, 2025)[14].

Slash Utilization, Strategically

Pay revolving balances early (before the statement closes) so a lower balance reports (Fair Isaac Corporation, 2025)[14]. If needed, request credit-limit increases on long-standing accounts with clean history (Consumer Financial Protection Bureau, 2023)[7].

Preserve Account Age

Keep your oldest, no-fee cards open (MyFICO, 2025)[26]. If you must simplify, close the newest accounts first (Fair Isaac Corporation, 2025)[14].

Be Surgical With New Credit

Batch rate-shopping for auto or mortgage within a short window (Fair Isaac Corporation, 2025)[14]. Avoid opening multiple new revolving accounts within 6–12 months of a mortgage application (Consumer Financial Protection Bureau, 2023)[7].

Build a "Thick" File Over Time

Aim for a healthy mix: at least 2–3 major credit cards, one installment loan paid as agreed, and (when appropriate) a mortgage (Fair Isaac Corporation, 2025)[14]. Never rush; build patiently (MyFICO, 2025)[26].

Don't Use Debt as Income

If you can't pay cash, don't buy it—exception: a reasonably-priced home aligned with your long-term plan (Bankrate, 2025)[27]. Treat cars as expenses, not investments; keep terms short (Consumer Financial Protection Bureau, 2023)[7].

Plan for Resilience

Keep an emergency fund so a job loss or medical event doesn't turn into lates, collections, and score damage (Federal Reserve, 2024)[1].

Escalate When Necessary

If you suspect discrimination or can't resolve errors, document everything and file complaints with the CFPB (Consumer Financial Protection Bureau, 2023)[7]; for housing/credit issues, speak with a HUD-approved counselor (U.S. Department of Housing and Urban Development, 2025)[55].

Track Both FICO and Vantage

Many apps show VantageScore; mortgage lenders may use older FICO versions (MyFICO, 2025)[26]. Track both to avoid surprises (Fair Isaac Corporation, 2025)[14].

CHAPTER 4
REPAIRING DAMAGED CREDIT

"We may encounter many defeats, but we must not be defeated."

Maya Angelou

Your credit score is an essential aspect of your financial life. Most creditors will determine the loan amount you are approved for based on your credit score (Fair Isaac Corporation, 2025)[14]. If you've had a loan application denied in the past, it may be connected to your overall credit rating.

Many credit users fail to understand that terrible credit habits carry serious consequences. Poor credit habits are not only a breach of your credit contract; they also raise concerns over your money management habits. To lenders, a poor credit report indicates that you are living beyond your means or on credit cards, and now you are applying for more credit than you can handle responsibly (Consumer Financial Protection Bureau, 2023)[7].

These two areas should be monitored closely because your consumer debt, not including your mortgage, should be at most 20% of your annual income. Keeping this at 20% is how you keep your debt-to-income ratio low (Bankrate, 2025)[27]. Lenders will deny your loan if your debt-to-income ratio is too high, and they will deny your loan if they feel you have too much debt in relation to your income.

As stated above, your credit score may be the difference between you and some of the best interest rates on auto loans, mortgages, and utilities (Federal Reserve Bank of New York, 2023)[9]. To get great deals on these, aim for a credit score above 740.

Put simply, a good credit score is the reward you receive for financial responsibility. And this may be relatively easy to earn if you try not to live above your means and pay your bills on time. However, life happens. And for many reasons, even the most responsible humans may not always have the best credit scores.

9 Common Credit Mistakes that can Cost you Money and Lose Points on Your Score.

1. Reserving Credit Cards for Emergencies

Some card users reserve certain credit cards for emergencies; a particular card is left unused and reserved as a safety net. A reserved and unused card may fail to work when needed. It would help if you used it occasionally, and when you do, pay it off immediately. Also, if you do not maintain a good credit score, they may cancel your card or significantly reduce your credit limit (Consumer Financial Protection Bureau, 2023)[7].

Imagine what could happen if someone with bad intentions gains access to your unused card's details. Not only that, but an unused card can be a liability for you and your credit card company. It could spell trouble, and you may be left to make payments for purchases you know nothing about. It may even be more challenging to do anything about it, as you do not receive bills monthly with the card and may, therefore, take a while to detect the fraud—by then, the fraudster would be long gone without a single trail.

Instead of leaving a card unused for emergencies, a better thing to do would be to set up a savings account if you have not already. This way, there will be cash to live on in an emergency and zero bills to pay once you are back on your feet. If you still decide to leave a card for emergencies, activate regular/monthly bills by making small monthly purchases that you pay off immediately.

2. Filing for Bankruptcy

When struggling with financial issues, it may seem like picking the lesser of two evils at the time, but this can destroy your credit, and unfortunately, most people who take that route don't realize this (Federal Trade Commission, 2023)[45].

If you must file for bankruptcy, ensure all other options, such as consumer credit counseling and debt consolidation, have been exhausted. Filing for bankruptcy should be a last resort and should come only after a financial advisor recommends it. Several free financial counselors are available, and you should use their services before filing for bankruptcy (Consumer Financial Protection Bureau, 2023)[7].

While filing for bankruptcy sounds so simple, in reality, this seemingly simple and innocent action could devastate your credit score and limit your general financial choices. If you are at the point where you believe filing bankruptcy is the only choice you have, then you should be placing calls right now to get a second opinion—preferably from an expert.

For help and more information, go to Hud.gov (U.S. Department of Housing and Urban Development, 2025)[55]. There are local housing counselors in your community who can advise you on your best options.

3. Paying your Credit Card Bills Late

Paying your credit card bill late is terrible, but completely ignoring payment is the biggest disservice you could do to your credit rating. This includes defaulting on loans, evading bill collectors, or forgetting or pretending to forget an unpaid account entirely. You only worsen things; the longer it goes on, the greater the damage will be to your credit report and financial future (Consumer Financial Protection Bureau, 2023)[7].

Defaulting on loans and having your accounts go into collections are some of the worst ways you can harm your credit. Creditors will eventually give up on trying to contact you, and they'll sell your debts to third parties/debt collectors specialized in using whatever means possible to ensure you pay back what you owe.

Offenses such as these will crush your credit score and remain stamped on your credit report and financial history for a long time (Federal Trade Commission, 2023)[45]. You may later pay off these balances or somehow forget they exist, but they will make sure you remember your mistake.

4. Not Keeping Track of your Utilization Score

This is a little tricky, but it can be simplified. One of the critical things creditors look at is your "credit utilization rate." Your "credit utilization rate" is essentially how much credit is available to you versus how much you use (Fair Isaac Corporation, 2025)[14]. For example, imagine you have a card with a ten-thousand-dollar limit and charge nine thousand dollars on it. Your credit utilization would be 90 percent.

You may think, "Hey, what does it matter? I'm still within my credit limit." Well, it does matter: You should always aim for a low credit utilization rate. Canceling a zero balance account could cause your credit utilization rate to skyrocket, dropping your overall credit score.

If you have a second card with a ten thousand limit and a zero balance, your total credit would be $20,000, putting your utilization rate at less than 50 percent. Always keep older zero balance accounts open when possible to have a considerable credit history to your name (MyFICO, 2025)[26].

5. Closing Old Accounts

Canceling old credit accounts affects your credit history by making it seem shorter. The length of your credit history makes up 15 percent of your credit score (Fair Isaac Corporation, 2025)[14]. If there are no annual charges, the cards should be left open because you have nothing to lose.

6. Having an Account Sent to Collections

Please pay attention to your credit payments to avoid creditors sending third-party debt collectors after you collect payments. Your account might be sent to collections before you are charged off. The collection status signifies that your creditor gave up on getting back payments after every effort ended in futility and thus was left with no option other than sending the debt-collecting organization after you (Consumer Financial Protection Bureau, 2023)[7]. Communicate with your creditors to avoid this from happening. Make payment arrangements that fit your budget, and eventually, your debt will be paid over time. Patience is the key. You didn't develop derogatory credit overnight, so repairing it will not happen overnight.

7. Having an Account Charge Off

When it becomes clear to creditors that you would be defaulting on payment, your account is charged off. A charge-off does not mean you are no longer responsible for your debt; it simply means they've given up on getting you to pay them directly (Federal Trade Commission, 2023)[45].

This is one of the worst things that can happen to your credit because as soon as your account is charged off, you cannot make any purchases with that credit card. You still owe the charged-off amount, but your creditor will report your charged-off status to the credit bureaus (Consumer Financial Protection Bureau, 2023)[7]. This status will remain in your records for seven years from the date the account went delinquent.

If in the future you request credit, your credit report will be reviewed, and creditors and lenders will see you've had a charge-off. Many unsecured creditors will not approve a loan with an open charge-off. Even if they do, you can expect higher-than-normal interest, fees, and short terms to repay.

8. Applying for Too Many Credit Cards or Credit Lines

Of your total credit score, credit inquiries account for about 10 percent (Fair Isaac Corporation, 2025)[14]. Having too many loan and credit card applications in a single period will cause a drop in your total credit rating. Where possible, cut down on your credit applications. If you need a loan, shop for it within a given period. Depending on the lender's credit score, this shopping window may range from 14 to 45 days (MyFICO, 2025)[26]. Limit it to 14 days.

To stay on the safe side, keep your search focused and brief. One loan inquiry has less effect on your credit score than frequent searches for new lines of credit.

9. Errors on your Credit Report

Get in the habit of requesting your credit report at least once a year (Annual Credit Report, 2025)[51]. You can obtain one free of charge from each of the three leading credit agencies. Examining your credit records can help you identify and correct errors in social security numbers or names; people with common names may suffer surcharges that do not apply or could even identify fraud. Correcting these errors may improve your credit score (Consumer Financial Protection Bureau, 2023)[7].

Before you begin, understand that there is no such thing as a quick fix for credit. For some, credit repair companies can be the go-to organizations for credit repair, but the fact is that there is nothing they can offer to repair your damaged credit that you cannot do yourself. Save your money. You need the extra money to pay the debt and a good credit repair firm to remove the creditors.

HERE ARE 8 STEPS TO REPAIRING YOUR CREDIT

1. Get Copies of Your Credit Reports

Before making any repair attempts on your damaged credit, you should know what you are out to repair. You are entitled to free annual reports from the three major credit bureaus, Experian, Equifax, and TransUnion (Annual Credit Report, 2025)[51], and read through each report for negatives that may be weighing down your credit ratings.

2. Understand The Credit Information You Need to Repair

The actions you will need to take may include:

- Finding delinquent accounts and maxed out credit accounts.
- Identifying wrong account information, identity mix-ups, and incorrectly reported payments.
- Highlight the information to make a credit payment plan.
- Notify your credit agency regarding incorrect or wrongly presented details (Consumer Financial Protection Bureau, 2023)[7].

3. Order All Three Credit Reports

Lenders and creditors may report to only one of the credit bureaus. Since these bureaus rarely share information, there is always the possibility of discovering conflicting information in each report (Consumer Financial Protection Bureau, 2023)[7]. With all three reports, you get a full view of your credit record, and you can proceed to repair each report from the different bureaus instead of working on just one.

Make an extra copy of each report if you need to dispute the records. If you need to file a dispute, send one copy to the credit bureau and keep the other.

4. Spread Disputes Over a Period of Time

Take your time to begin all your disputes at once. If there are inconsistencies, you need to dispute in your credit report, dispute only one per letter, and ensure they are sufficiently spaced out. You could stir up suspicions on your credit if you file too many disputes at once (Consumer Financial Protection Bureau, 2023)[7].

5. Arrange to Catch Up on Your Payments

Your payment history is the most significant determinant of your credit score (Fair Isaac Corporation, 2025)[14]. You can only improve your credit situation if you are up in your payments; you must get current on all accounts before you start the process.

Contact your creditor/lenders if you cannot bring all payments current to make payment arrangements to get current over time.

Ensure you are open with your creditors about your situation, including details on how much you can afford to pay and how long you intend to take to pay it (Consumer Financial Protection Bureau, 2023)[7].

Most creditors are willing to work out a mutually agreeable payment plan. Suppose your creditors are indifferent to your request for a reasonable payment plan. In that case, you should consult a consumer credit counselor to help you negotiate better terms and get back on track.

6. Use a Secured Card

Using a secured card to make a few months of timely payments is an excellent way to start. For this, try out store cards, as they are comparatively easy to qualify. Pay off each balance entirely and on time each month, and you can then try applying for a regular credit card in six to twelve months (MyFICO, 2025)[26].

You can also see if your bank will allow you to open a secured credit account. This account type, like the store cards, requires you to deposit money equal to the credit limit the bank can fall back on if you miss a payment. This eliminates the bank's risk, so it may be easier to get a credit card. A co-signer is another option to build credit quickly.

7. Continue to Protect Yourself from Identity Theft

You are trying to revive a damaged credit score, and the last thing you want is to get plunged into fresh debt courtesy of identity thieves. To protect yourself from identity fraud, consider contacting the major credit bureaus to place a security freeze on your credit for free (Annual Credit Report, 2025)[51]. This way, a new line of credit can only be opened in your name once you unfreeze it.

8. Eliminate unhealthy financial habits

You should see your credit improve within two to three months. In extreme cases, improvement will only be noticed after a few years.

This, of course, will be determined by the extent of damage suffered by your credit.

Live within your means. Show me a person with a budget, and I will show you a person with excellent credit. Having a credit card should not tempt you to charge purchases you would not usually buy. Set aside an emergency fund and save money for significant expenses in the future (Federal Reserve, 2024)[1]. If you do this, you may never have to skip payments, and you will have something tangible to fall back on if you ever find yourself in financial duress.

Even when your credit is fully repaired, hold on to the valuable habits you formed and the lessons you learned during the repairing process. That way, maintaining your brand-new credit history will be easier.

Remember, setbacks are part of the process, and your credit score can drop without warning. This in no way implies that you did anything wrong. Keep at the process, and your credit score will improve over time. There are algorithms at work that you need to have control over.

Follow the steps outlined above, and you'll be on your way to a better credit score. But be patient. Your credit wasn't damaged overnight, so expect credit repair to take time. Just keep at it, and you'll be rewarded in the long run with better rates and a great deal of cash in interest savings.

CHAPTER 5

DISPUTING CREDIT REPORT INFORMATION

"Without hard work, nothing grows but weeds."

Gordon B. Hinckley

A report from the Federal Trade Commission says that one in five American consumers have errors on their credit reports (Federal Trade Commission, 2023)[45]. While hopefully, you're never the one person among the five, anyone can have the wrong information on their credit report. The good news is that it can be corrected because inconsistencies are commonplace and can be resolved by filing a dispute.

If, on the other hand, you happen to be part of the 35 percent of Americans who have never checked their credit report for errors or the 14 percent who do so less than once a year, then you may want to rethink that and request your credit report as soon as you can!

CHECK YOUR CREDIT REPORT FOR ERRORS ANNUALLY

To find credit report errors, first, get a free credit report. You are entitled to a free report from each credit reporting bureau once a year through annualcreditreport.com (Annual Credit Report, 2025)[51]. You are also entitled to a free report if you receive government assistance/welfare, are unemployed and looking to get a job soon, or have stolen your identity.

Check the laws in your state to see if you qualify for a free credit report. If you don't, you can request one directly from the credit bureaus for ten to twenty dollars, depending on the bureau or state.

Carefully check your report for errors. If you discover any, confirm that they are errors from the credit reporting bureaus or the information provider (Consumer Financial Protection Bureau, 2023)[7]. You don't want to file a dispute and later discover that you made the payment or purchase.

HAVE THE SUPPORTING DOCUMENTATION READY

If you are sure you have found a factual error, highlight it on the report and then put together any documents (e.g., proof of payment) that can lend credence to your case.

Tell the credit bureau the details you believe need to be corrected. The three credit reporting bureaus will let you file a credit report dispute online or via mail or phone (Consumer Financial Protection Bureau, 2023)[7].

Let the creditor or information provider know you are filing a dispute over the information they gave to the credit reporting bureau. If the inconsistency originated from how your credit details were reported to the credit bureau, you may need to write a similar letter explaining the error.

FILING A CREDIT REPORT DISPUTE

How is a credit report dispute filed? First, understand that you can dispute your credit report in several ways.

3 WAYS TO DISPUTE YOUR CREDIT REPORT

1. Online: You can get access to your credit report and file a dispute through any of the online dispute centers of the three major credit reporting bureaus (Consumer Financial Protection Bureau, 2023)[7]. You do not need a dispute number to file a dispute through an online dispute center.

2. Over a phone call: You can submit a dispute by calling the number displayed on your credit report. Call the number on your credit report if you already have the paper copy of your report, and reference the report number for quicker access. Ensure you keep a record of when you called, the agent you spoke to, and every detail you were offered concerning your dispute.

3. By Mail: You can also dispute by writing a letter to any of the three credit reporting agencies (Consumer Financial Protection Bureau, 2023)[7]:

The following page contains a dispute letter template from the Federal Trade Commission (Federal Trade Commission, 2023)[45] that you can use to write your credit report dispute letter.

Credit Dispute Letter

Jane Smith, — [Your Name]
1234 First Street — [Street Address]
Los Angeles, CA 91602 — [City, State, Zip Code]
Complaint Department — [Company Name]

Dear Sir or Madam:

I am writing to dispute the following information in my file. I have circled the items I dispute on the attached copy of the report I received.

This item [identify item(s) disputed by name of source, such as creditors or tax court, and identify type of item, such as credit account, judgment, etc.] is [inaccurate or incomplete] because [describe what is inaccurate or incomplete and why]. I am requesting that the item be removed [or request another specific change] to correct the information.

Enclosed are copies of [use this sentence if applicable and describe any enclosed documentation, such as payment records and court documents] supporting my position. Please reinvestigate this [these] matter[s] and [delete or correct] the disputed item[s] as soon as possible.

Sincerely,

Your name

Enclosures: — [List what you are enclosing.]

WHICH "ERRORS" CAN YOU DISPUTE?

While you can file a dispute for any "error" at all, you must understand that the credit bureau will only delete details required to be deleted from your report by the law (Federal Trade Commission, 2023)[45]. Even before any deletion is done, an investigation will be carried out to verify your claims. Once that is done, you should look for any suspicious-looking information or credit lines you do not remember opening.

Here are some common errors you can and should dispute when they appear on your credit report:

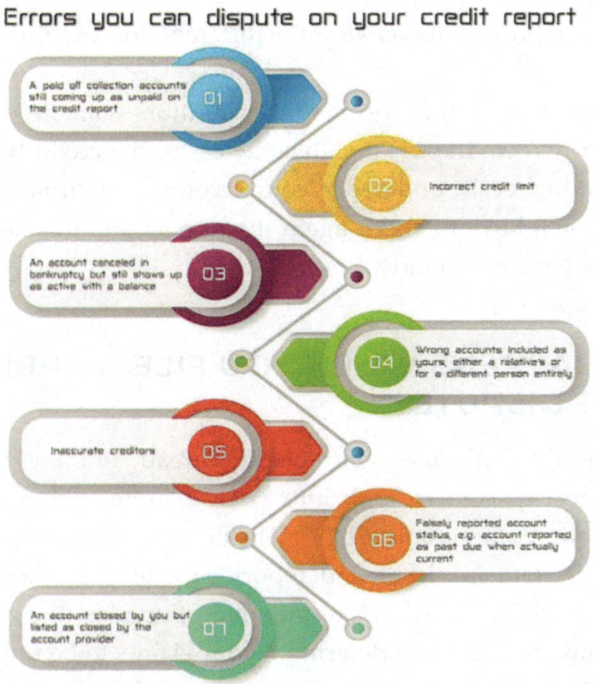

- Paid-off collection accounts are still showing as unpaid on the credit report.
- An inaccurate credit limit
- An account was canceled in bankruptcy but still shows as active with a balance.
- Wrong accounts included as yours (either a relative's or for a different person entirely)
- Inaccurate creditor information
- A False reported account status, e.g., an account reported as past due when current.
- An account is closed by you but listed as closed by the provider.

If you find any incorrect information during a routine credit report check, you should question it (Consumer Financial Protection Bureau, 2023)[7]. Not all three major credit reporting bureaus show the exact credit details on their reports. So, it should be no surprise that your TransUnion report contains slightly different information than your Equifax.

The dissimilarity may be because creditors sometimes report to only one or two credit bureaus. In some cases, the credit bureaus may not have all the recent updates of your account in your latest report; in this case, you'll have to check again three to six months later to see if the updates have been made.

WHAT HAPPENS WHEN YOU FILE A CREDIT REPORT DISPUTE?

When you file a dispute, your credit bureau and the information provider are expected to look into your dispute within thirty days (Federal Trade Commission, 2023)[45]. The bureau will forward the documents to the data furnisher and report back to you, except in cases where your claims may be unfounded. Suppose the information provider and credit bureau determine your claims to be unfounded. In that case, they can decide not to investigate as long as you're notified of the decision within five days.

Also, while it is expected to find "incredible" claims on the internet of consumers clearing their credit reports of negative unpaid debt through credit repair, you must be wary of filing pointless credit report disputes. The Fair Credit Reporting Act (Federal Trade Commission, 2023)[45] covers many things for the consumer, including requiring that consumers' disputes are actively and immediately investigated; it ensures that abuse is minimized by offering these credit bureaus some rights.

If you are still waiting to hear back from either or both entities after thirty days, call or check online to know what may be holding up the process. Suppose you still do not get a satisfactory answer or feel both entities may deliberately and wrongfully ignore your request. In that case, you may need to involve the Consumer Financial Protection Bureau (Consumer Financial Protection Bureau, 2023)[7] or file a complaint with the Better Business Bureau.

If all goes well and your claims are validated, the credit reporting bureau will provide you with the results of the investigation once completed. You will also get a new copy of your credit report if changes are effected. Additionally, you can request that the credit bureau send a notification to every creditor, employer, or any other body that had accessed your credit rating in the months before you filed the dispute (Consumer Financial Protection Bureau, 2023)[7].

DISPUTES AND MORTGAGE

When applying for a mortgage, you should be careful when disputing an item on your credit report. You may be unable to close on a mortgage with an open dispute. As disputes take quite some time to get resolved, you will eventually be forced to wait out the dispute period, time you may not have to spare. This is another primary reason why you should regularly monitor your credit report.

STAY IN THE KNOW

Even though filing and going through the dispute process may be challenging, especially for busy individuals with jam-packed schedules, you already know your credit health is something you should never handle with laxity. One or two errors could be the difference between you and low-interest rates, mortgages, or any other credit product.

You have all the tools required to dispute a credit report. Again, if you have not or do not check your credit report each time you receive one, you should rethink this and request a free copy (Annual Credit Report, 2025)[51]. Be a savvy consumer. Don't just accept credit details you cannot recognize but are included in your report. Spot and report the errors and save money on all your credit products.

One of the very first obstacles you might face is your credit score. You may be looking to purchase a brand-new car or get a mortgage on a magnificent house. Of course, if your credit score is too low, your dreams of getting those beautiful luxuries may never get actualized. As such, you need to get familiar with the concept of section 609, as it may serve as a lifeline in most cases.

HOW CAN I WORK WITH 609 TO FILE A DISPUTE?

According to the Federal Trade Commission's research in the United States, one in every four individuals has discovered mistakes in their credit reports (Federal Trade Commission, 2023)[45].

However, section 609 of the Fair Credit Reporting Act (FCRA) (Federal Trade Commission, 2023)[45] deals with your right to obtain copies of your credit reports and the information contained therein. Surprisingly, Section 609 has nothing to do with your request to question or dispute your credit report data or the requirement of a credit reporting organization to investigate your objections.

Although a section of the FCRA outlines your rights to dispute information on your credit reports, it is not found in section 609. Instead, Section 611 of the Act contains this information (Federal Trade Commission, 2023)[45]. With section 611, it is possible to challenge the information you believe is false. The disputed data must be discarded if it can't be authenticated or confirmed.

In other words, the (Fair Credit Reporting Act) FCRA (Federal Trade Commission, 2023)[45] gives reporting agencies no legal authority to conceal your personal information from you.

It is valid to know that, thanks to section 611, we all have the right to challenge information that we feel is inaccurate or unverifiable. If the disputed data can't be verified or validated, it has to be deleted.

While several people have attempted to file a complaint with the Federal Trade Commission (FTC) concerning their credit reports, they have all gotten a declarative statement from the FTC stating that the agency will not assist in any disagreement between a consumer and a credit bureau. Most times, this kind of statement means you're on your own. As a result, many people have resorted to submitting dispute letters using Section 609 or engaging a lawyer to assist them in their battles with the credit bureaus.

A properly written and organized 609 dispute letter can provide results where other techniques have failed. You must follow specific steps to obtain the best results during your letter-writing process. The process may be extended and bureaucratic, but it is worth it.

HERE ARE 7 STEPS TO GET YOU STARTED:

1. Obtaining Your Credit Reports

Before writing your letter:

- Obtain copies of your credit report from all three credit bureaus - Experian, TransUnion, and Equifax (Annual Credit Report, 2025)[51].
- Check for any incorrect and negative items.
- Double-check to ensure that all the listed debts are accurate.

Having your reports allows you to refer to them precisely in your letter.

2. Reference Section 609 of the FCRA

The most crucial thing to remember when composing your disagreement letter is to refer to the FCRA and specifically Section 609 of it (Federal Trade Commission, 2023)[45].

In your letter, include a statement stating that you exercise your right under the Fair Credit Reporting Act, Section 609, and ask for all information about debts in your credit report. You are entitled to all documentation about each item, including the original credit application and any signed contract.

3. Request for Removal

In your letter, remember to include a statement informing the credit bureau that if they cannot verify an item in your credit report by finding the original contract or other files required to validate it, they must remove that item within 30 days (Federal Trade Commission, 2023)[45].

4. Mail Your 609 Letter and Request Receipt of Delivery

Once you've created your letter and mailed it, ensure to request a delivery receipt from the United States Postal Service. You will receive a delivery receipt as soon as your mail is delivered. By doing this, the Credit Bureau cannot claim that your letter was not received.

5. Save and Make copies of Your Documents

It is essential to keep an organized record of your whole dispute process. Make a copy of your letter for future purposes, note important dates and events, such as when the letter was sent and received, and keep any associated files organized. You can achieve this by either backing up your e-copy to an external storage or storing them safely if you also have hard copies.

6. Attach a Proof of Identification

With every correspondence you send, always include proof of your identity. As per section 610 (a) (i) of the FCRA (Federal Trade Commission, 2023)[45], consumers must present "valid identification" to get a response from a credit bureau.

When you write your letter correctly, you'll get improved credit scores. Although you can create and send a 609 letter independently, obtaining expert guidance from a credit repair lawyer or credit counselor is always a good idea, especially if you're unfamiliar with the formal procedure. Lawyers and counselors can help you with the 609 letters, any subsequent dispute letters, and other elements of your debt relief and credit restoration efforts.

7. Proceed to Write Your Letter

Once you have all the required information, it's time to draft your letter. Clarity and an eye for detail are the secrets to writing an effective dispute letter.

WHAT DO I NEED TO INCLUDE IN MY DISPUTE LETTER?

Your 609 dispute letter is your last resort to improve your credit score or erase a credit record you are uncomfortable with. As a result, your letter must contain certain "ingredients" if you want it to receive an answer from the credit bureau and ultimately serve its intended purpose of enhancing your credit score.

You must present valid identification to receive a response from any credit bureau, according to Section 610 of the FCRA (Federal Trade Commission, 2023)[45]. However, every 609 letters should be accompanied by documents (i.e., a photocopy of your social security card or driver's license) proving your identity.

Here are some of the documents you should note and include in your dispute letter before sending it:

- Your full name
- Contact information
- Your social security number
- Date of Birth
- The credit report with the account highlighted
- Your driver's license, passport or other state-issued identification
- Your name and address on a rental agreement, mortgage contract, or utility bill

Ensure that you point out the specific issue in your report. Ask the credit bureau to look into it and confirm that it is correct. Maintain a clean, concise, and precise style in your writing.

For instance, you can try sending something like:

"I'm requesting information on [report] shown on my consumer credit report [account number] under the Fair Credit Reporting Act, especially section 609. I am entitled to access the primary source of information in the original contract that bears my signature, as per section 609."

Remind the credit agency that they must remove the information from your credit report if it cannot be validated with documentation from the creditor (Federal Trade Commission, 2023)[45]. Be polite and assertive in your writing. End your letter with something like this:

"As mentioned earlier, if you are unable to provide me with the documentation to validate the information, please correct the error as soon as possible. Thank you."

WHEN SENDING YOUR 609 LETTERS, MAKE COPIES OF ALL DOCUMENTS OF IDENTITY

Never send your actual ID, passport, social security number, or any other information. To keep track of your records, you'll need to make copies. Sending original identifications over the mail can lead to identity theft, which you'll not like to experience.

IF YOU'RE MAILING A 609 LETTER, MAKE SURE TO RECEIVE AND KEEP A COPY OF THE DELIVERY RECEIPT.

Credit bureaus must investigate properly written requests within 30 to 45 days (Federal Trade Commission, 2023)[45]. With the receipt, you can monitor your letter, guarantee it reaches the bureau, and check its response time. Here's a fun fact about what a 609 letter is and how it might benefit you:

Suppose the credit agency doesn't respond to you within the required time frame, and you have the delivery receipt. You have the right to demand that they remove the wrong information immediately based on your evidence.

It is important to note that you can ask for a detailed account of the investigative process. This means you can request information from the credit bureaus' databases. If you're contacted by the credit agency by telephone, do not verify any information over the phone. The burden of proof is on the credit agency to verify the debt. They must honor your request to send proof of their claim.

CHAPTER 6
CREDIT UTILIZATION

"I am not a product of circumstances.
I am a product of my decisions."
Stephen Covey

In this chapter, we will discuss credit utilization in detail and how, if used correctly, it can keep your credit healthy. In business, utilization is the term that applies to the partial use of the line of credit to maintain good business relationships with third parties, especially when funds are unavailable to pay for products or services paid for with checks.

However, it has been proven that using your credit card has the same effect and can help keep your credit healthy (Fair Isaac Corporation, 2025)[14]. You can compare it to a savings account: Instead of spending all your savings, you can take what you need to address a problem so that you have some money left for new issues that may come in the future.

AS A GENERAL RULE, THE FORMULA TO QUALIFY BORROWERS IS THE FOLLOWING:

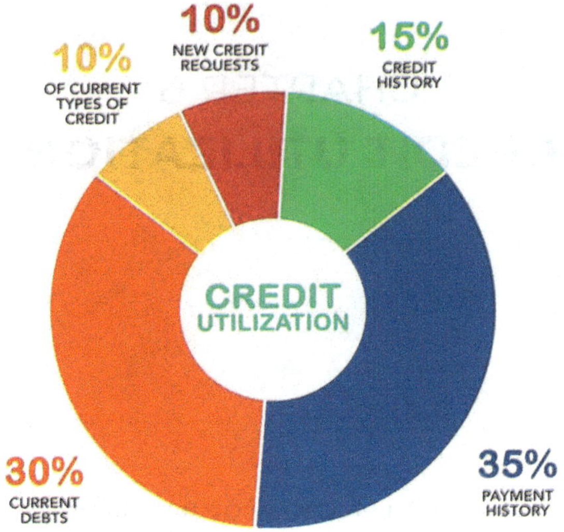

CREDIT FORMULA FOR BUYERS

Given that your current debts should be no more than 30 percent of your total credit limit, credit utilization is a good way for you to "control" your credit score (MyFICO, 2025)[26]. This does not include my belief that your total consumer debt (not mortgages) should not be more than 10% of your annual income. All consumer debt is bad debt. Try to keep it at zero.

Keep in mind that a zero balance is a recommendation, not a rule. Credit rating agencies can use different standards, but most believe that maintaining an average debt balance of 30 percent of your limit reflects healthy finances (Fair Isaac Corporation, 2025)[14].

What does "utilization" of 30 percent mean? Let's say you have a credit card with a limit set at $4,500, 30% utilization means that your average debt balance should be at most $1,350, and preferably you should not exceed that amount with any expense.

This principle applies globally. For example, if you have three credit cards, and among them, you can access $17,000, your total debt between all three credit cards should be at most $5,100. Understanding this point is not complicated, but it's another thing altogether to put it into practice. To successfully practice "utilization" to improve your credit score, the following tips may help you.

5 WAYS TO PRACTICE UTILIZATION TO IMPROVE YOUR CREDIT SCORE

1. Record how much you are charging on each card.

Acquire the habit of periodically checking your accounts online to control expenses; to be close to using the 30 percent credit limit on one card, making a payment, or using another card (MyFICO, 2025)[26]. Some qualifying formulas penalize exceeding 30 percent of utilization, so try to keep your balances below that margin.

2. Set up balance alerts. If you are one of those people who forget everything, ask your issuer to send alerts via SMS or email to indicate when you are close to 30 percent of the use of your card. You could set the alert when you reach 20 percent, so you can plan before you reach 30 percent.

3. Increase credit limits on your cards.

If, despite keeping payments up to date, your expenses do not allow you to be below 30 percent of the usage, then request an increase in the credit limit. For example, if you have used $2,000 on a $4,000 card, your utilization is 50 percent. If you double the credit limit to $8,000, then your utilization will be only 25 percent (Fair Isaac Corporation, 2025)[14]. This measure can affect the qualification in principle, but in a short time, it can be recovered.

4. Find out when your issuer reports to the rating agencies.

All issuers send your records to the rating agencies once a month, and the date doesn't necessarily coincide with the closing date of your payment cycle (Consumer Financial Protection Bureau, 2023)[7]. Communicate with your issuer and ask them what date they send your records. This way, you can make your payments at the right time and improve your rating.

5. Get in the habit of paying mid-cycle.

Getting into the habit of paying your cards twice a month instead of once might be enough to improve the "utilization" rate. Reducing payment periods from thirty to fifteen days can help you stay close to the 30 percent rate recommended by qualifiers (MyFICO, 2025)[26]. A useful tool may be to schedule two automatic payments per month.

You will keep your credit score healthy as long as you have good payment habits and stay below 30 percent of your utilization (Fair Isaac Corporation, 2025)[14].

Note: Scores close to 800 points usually belong to people who achieve utilization of just 7 percent of their credit (MyFICO, 2025)[26].

CHAPTER 7
HOW TO SURVIVE BANKRUPTCY

"Never, never, never give up."
~Winston Churchill

Going bankrupt can happen to anyone, including someone living from paycheck to paycheck. This savvy business owner has everything under control and even works two or more jobs. I am not an attorney, and if you are thinking about bankruptcy, I highly advise you to seek the advice of a licensed attorney who specializes in bankruptcy. Although I am not an attorney, I've had the experience of working with individuals and families who have filed for bankruptcy and are now working towards buying a home.

In this chapter, we will be exploring:

- What is bankruptcy?
- Why would anyone need to file for bankruptcy?
- What happens when you file for bankruptcy?

Bankruptcy is a legal process supervised by federal courts designed to help businesses and individuals clear out entire or part of their debts (Federal Trade Commission, 2023)[45]. It is a very sensitive and personal issue. Your whole life is on public display for the courts and the public to see. It causes emotional and family issues, and for many, it is seen as a personal and financial failure. But the truth is that it is not.

Bankruptcy has been a part of our history since the beginning of time. For many, it is the year of Jubilee, and it should be looked at as a new beginning and a time to start over. So don't be discouraged; be encouraged that you have a fresh opportunity to start over.

In bankruptcy, a judge or a court trustee examines the individuals' assets and liabilities and decides whether they are legally required to pay off their debts. If they qualify for bankruptcy, all or part of their debt is canceled.

A small percentage of cases are sometimes dismissed when the judge or court trustee, after a thorough examination, believes that the individuals can still pay off their debts.

You may wonder: Why would anyone file for bankruptcy if they can repay the debts owed? As unbelievable as it may seem, many people believe they can walk into a court and tell the story about their financial situation, and the court will sympathize with them and cancel their debt, but that is not the reality.

Individuals or married couples can file several types of bankruptcy, the most common being **Chapter 7, Chapter 11, and Chapter 13** (Federal Trade Commission, 2023)[45].

The most common of the three is **Chapter 7 bankruptcy**.

Chapter 7 may allow you to keep some essential assets termed "exempt" property, e.g., cars used for work, equipment, and social security income (Federal Trade Commission, 2023)[45]. "Non-exempt" assets, such as a second car, a second home, investments, cash, etc., are liquidated to pay off. There are income qualifications tied to family size. These income qualifications vary by state. Please consult a bankruptcy attorney for the details. You may still qualify by proving that after spending on the necessities, like rent and food, you will have very little or nothing left to pay off most of your unsecured debts. This could include personal loans, medical bills, credit cards, etc.

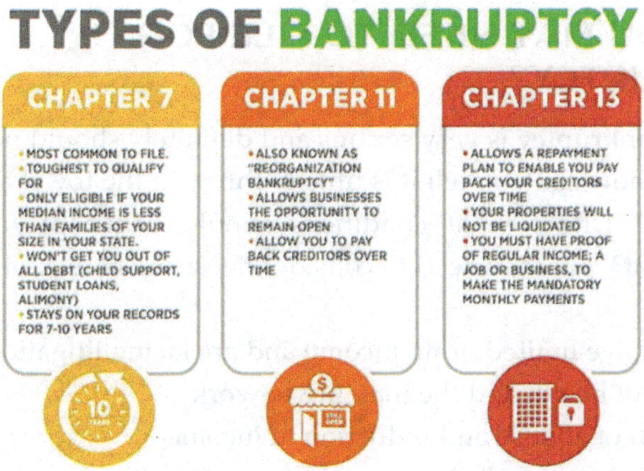

While filing for a Chapter 7 bankruptcy can cover much, it will not get you out of all debts. For example, court-ordered alimony, child support, or a student loan will not simply go away because you filed a Chapter 7 bankruptcy (U.S. Department of Education, 2024)[2]. Also note that, like other bankruptcies, Chapter 7 is included in your record for seven to ten years after you file (Federal Trade Commission, 2023)[45].

Chapter 11 bankruptcy ("reorganization bankruptcy") allows businesses to remain open while their debts and assets are restructured so they can pay back creditors. Although the company continues to operate throughout the bankruptcy proceedings, most critical decisions are only made with the court's approval.

Quite similar to Chapter 11 bankruptcy, **Chapter 13 bankruptcy** allows a repayment plan to enable you to pay back your creditors over time (Federal Trade Commission, 2023)[45]. Unlike Chapter 7 bankruptcy, your properties will not be liquidated, but the process could drag on for three to five years before your debts are discharged. To qualify, you must have proof of regular income (from a job or business) to make the mandatory monthly payments.

WHY YOU MAY NEED TO FILE FOR BANKRUPTCY?

Filing for bankruptcy is very serious and definitely should not be taken lightly. But how can you tell it is time to throw in the towel and declare bankruptcy? Under what conditions should bankruptcy become a viable option? You may need to consider declaring bankruptcy if:

- You have limited or no income and are facing litigation
- Loss of health and the inability to work
- Death of spouse and reduction of income
- Victim of natural disasters and no insurance

Suppose any of these circumstances represent your life right now. Please consult an attorney and consider bankruptcy. You may need a fresh start. If not, then seek out the help of a housing counselor. You can find them in your local area at hud.gov (U.S. Department of Housing and Urban Development, 2025)[55].

Again, you must remember that while bankruptcy can help you out of many situations, it is not a magic pill for curing out-of-control debt.

While declaring bankruptcy may seem appealing, it is not always pleasant. Before you decide whether to file, we have compiled below some of the upsides and downsides of filing for bankruptcy to help you better understand the factors involved and how your decision to file or not to file for bankruptcy can affect you.

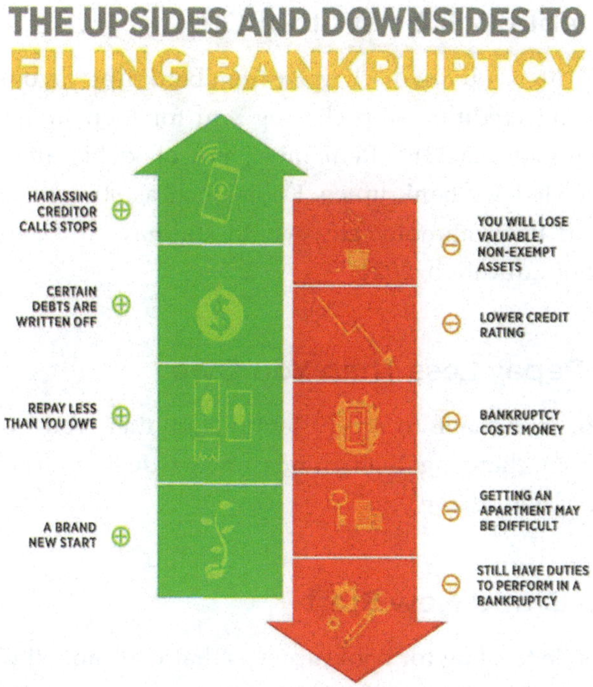

UPSIDES:

Harassing Creditor Calls Stop.

No one looks forward to getting regular calls from a single creditor. Think about how much stress you would undergo with so many creditors breathing down your neck and ringing your phone off the hook!

Once your bankruptcy filing is approved, you get immediate creditor protection (Federal Trade Commission, 2023)[45]. None of your creditors are permitted to contact you for debt collection or even take any action against you. This does not solve the issues on the ground, but you get peace and more clarity as you go through the bankruptcy process.

An administrator will be appointed to handle everything for you, including payments and communications with your creditors.

Certain Debts Will Be Written Off.

Immediately after you are discharged from bankruptcy, your debts are written off, and creditors stop chasing you for their money (Federal Trade Commission, 2023)[45]. Remember, not all debts are wiped out because you filed for bankruptcy. Debts such as student loans, child support, court fines, alimony, etc., would still have to be repaid (U.S. Department of Education, 2024)[2].

You May Repay Less Than You Owe.

Your creditors will have to accept less money than you owe and are forbidden from changing their minds once a deal is struck (Federal Trade Commission, 2023)[45].

You Get a Brand New Start.

Another upside to filing for bankruptcy is that you can tell when you'll be discharged. Thus, you will be able to draw up a credit rebuilding plan.

DOWNSIDES:

You Will Lose Valuable, Non-Exempt Assets

"Non-exempt assets," such as the equity ownership in your home, will likely be sold (Federal Trade Commission, 2023)[45]. Also, you will lose tax refunds for that year and any outstanding refunds from previous years. Business owners could also have their businesses sold and their staff laid off.

Lower Credit Rating.

Filing for bankruptcy will harm your credit rating (Fair Isaac Corporation, 2025)[14]. It will also remain on your report for seven to ten years after discharge (Federal Trade Commission, 2023)[45].

High Costs.

You will be charged for the entire bankruptcy process, including court fees and administrative charges, all from your assets.

Getting an Apartment May Be Difficult.

Some landlords may not allow you to rent their properties if you've declared bankruptcy.

You Still Have Duties to Perform in a Bankruptcy.

To get a bankruptcy discharge, you still need to perform some duties. These include regularly reporting your monthly income, attending credit counseling, making payments, and providing income tax information (Federal Trade Commission, 2023)[45].

HOW LONG AFTER A BANKRUPTCY BEFORE YOU CAN APPLY FOR A MORTGAGE?

Many wrongly believe filing bankruptcy eliminates their chances of qualifying for a mortgage. Wrong! You can apply and qualify for a mortgage as soon as one year after your discharge from bankruptcy, depending on the type of bankruptcy filed (U.S. Department of Housing and Urban Development, 2025)[55].

Generally, however, it is a good idea to wait until your credit rating bounces back to a reasonable level before you apply to increase your chances of qualifying.

The decision to file bankruptcy is never easy, but if you finally decide to go that route consult with a HUD approved housing counselor (U.S. Department of Housing and Urban Development, 2025)[55], and be certain that it is the right decision for you and your family.

FOUR STEPS TO RECOVERY:

1. Make Early Payments.

If you filed a Chapter 13 bankruptcy, draw up a budget and ensure you follow through on your repayment plan (Federal Trade Commission, 2023)[45]. Your credit report will reflect your payment history, influencing your credit score (Fair Isaac Corporation, 2025)[14]. Failure to make on-time payments will quickly hurt your credit score, especially considering you just got out of bankruptcy.

2. Open New Credit Lines.

New credit lines? Isn't that what got you there in the first place? And who gives a credit card to someone just fresh out of bankruptcy? Those are reasonable and valid questions, but understand this: To rebuild credit, you must take credit.

Several credit card issuers are willing to offer you a secured credit card even just a few months post-bankruptcy (Consumer Financial Protection Bureau, 2023)[7]. These cards come with lower-than-normal credit limits and higher-than-average interest rates, as you must provide a deposit in case you default.

You could start by opening up to three secured credit cards with $500 or more balances. Also, avoid carrying a balance and resist the urge to frequently apply for new credit, no matter how tempting the offer may seem, as every inquiry counts on your credit report (MyFICO, 2025)[26].

3. Save 10 Percent of Your Monthly Earnings.

Creditors need to know you are not in any financial distress and that you can be responsible with your finances. How do you prove this? Saving at least 10 percent of your monthly income immediately. Showing that you have reserves and are committed to no debt is the only way to prove to lenders that you will not repeat past mistakes (Federal Reserve, 2024)[1].

The goal is to have six months of your net monthly income in reserves as soon as possible. Once you have achieved this goal, do not take on significant debt. Use secured credit and pay off what you charge immediately. Never carry a balance.

4. Do Not Take on Any New Debt.

Avoid taking on new debt for any reason. At this point, any debt you take on is for the strategic reason of building credit. The limits will be low, which is okay. The goal is to stay debt-free and build credit at the same time (Consumer Financial Protection Bureau, 2023)[7].

Remember, if you must take on debt, it should be at most 10% of your annual income. This includes car loans and all consumer loans. If you need a car, borrow one from a family member with a vehicle they are not using or pay cash for a used car.

Filing for bankruptcy should never happen because you have allowed your debt to spiral out of control. If you follow these steps, not only will you be able to survive bankruptcy, but you will thrive financially.

CHAPTER 8
CREDIT REPAIR AGENCIES

"You can't cross the sea merely by standing and staring at the water."
Rabindranath Tagore

Many credit repair companies sell expensive services, claiming to be able to fix credit scores quickly. Buying into these claims is tempting because a good credit score is the primary requirement for getting a good loan, mortgage, or almost any other financing approval. You also already know a good credit score can cost or save you several thousand dollars in insurance premiums and interest (Fair Isaac Corporation, 2025)[14].

As credit repair companies gain new clients seeking to revive battered credit scores, it is only proper to know what the CFPB says about these companies before you use them. It should help you decide whether they are worth the money or hype. The CFPB's stance on credit repair companies is simple: There is nothing a credit repair agency can offer to renew your credit that you can't already do your-self (Consumer Financial Protection Bureau, 2023)[7].

Why do people seek their services? Sadly, most "credit fix seekers" are unaware they can do so themselves. Still, even people who do know they can fix their credit on their own are lured by the creative "pitches" of many credit repair companies and the usual too-good-to-be-true promises like boosting their credit score by 100 percent, reducing debt, and even scrubbing out the entire credit problem. Nothing could be further from the truth than that last statement, as something has to be wrong for default/damaging information to be removed.

"There are no ways to evade payments on true negatives—not even magic."

PROS AND CONS OF USING A CREDIT REPAIR COMPANY:

Some of these organizations have lived up to some claims, but many have also been involved in law suits related to their bogus offers and claims. Yes, they are not all totally "bad." Using them, however, comes with some pros and cons you should consider before buying whatever they may be "selling." On the other hand, repairing your credit is certainly not a walk in the park. There are pros and cons to taking up the process yourself, too. So, we'll examine some ways a credit repairer may help you more than you may be able to help yourself.

PROS:

They Have Familiarity and Experience.

Most credit agencies have had practical years of experience and resources to help you fix a bad credit score (Consumer Financial Protection Bureau, 2023)[7]. They know the ropes and can work directly with your lenders to help you come out of a bad debt.

They Are Respected.

Expectedly, long years of practice and affiliation with a reputable credit repair company often earn the credit repair officer's respect in the field. As a result, they can almost always bank on their familiarity with decision-makers at credit reporting, collections, and lending agencies, get taken seriously and negotiate advantageous deals.

They Are Hired for Results.

Credit companies are paid for results; reputable credit repair companies often state the scope of service and the fees required. As a result, they are usually compelled to work hard and fast to ensure significant improvements in their credit scores and get paid for the work done. But remember, there are no guarantees that any changes will take place.

They Are Time Savers.

If you are unfamiliar with credit law—as most are—such as the Fair Debt Collection Act and the Fair Credit Billing Act (Federal Trade

Commission, 2023)[45], you may likely spend some time researching and understanding these laws and how they can be managed to help people with credit issues like you. The experts in credit repair companies already know even the most minor details and how to use them to your benefit. The credit repair process, therefore, will be completed much faster than you can do on your own.

CONS:

You Play By Their Rules

Most credit repair organizations run on specific rules that cannot be changed for you or anyone else. As part of their repair process, credit organizations may need you to abide by their rules, like letting them be in charge of your spending habits/routines. Some may also require that you do not get any loans while they are working for you. While some people have no problem accepting these rules, others may have trouble with them.

Results Are Not Guaranteed

Before hiring a credit agency's services, remember that paying for the service is no guarantee that you will get the desired results (Consumer Financial Protection Bureau, 2023)[7]. Thankfully, some credit repair agencies abide by the CFDB rules and do not charge before results are seen. Others even offer a money-back guarantee. No legitimate repair company can guarantee that any changes will take place; all they can do is do the work and hope for the best.

You Can Get Scammed

There's always the possibility of getting scammed by a credit report company. Under the Credit Repair Organizations Act (Federal Trade Commission, 2023)[45], credit companies are forbidden from requesting payments until the services promised are completed. A big red flag would be credit companies or individuals that offer you a guarantee of a brand new credit file when they are finished. You should, therefore, be very aware of your rights as a consumer.

BENEFITS OF REPAIRING YOUR OWN CREDIT

If it ever comes down to it, understand that you are completely capable of fixing your own credit score at no cost if you go about it the right way. The following are some of the benefits you enjoy from doing it all yourself.

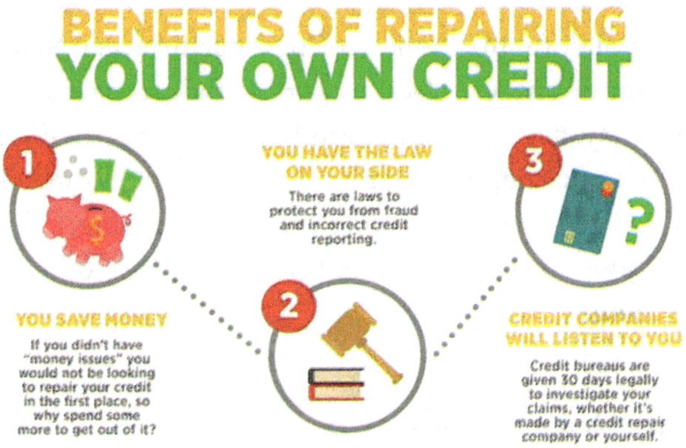

You Save Money.

If you didn't have "money issues," you would not be looking to repair your credit in the first place. So why spend even more to get out of it? At this point, it is safe to assume that while money is tight, you may have a surplus of time; you may as well invest some of that time into your own credit repair. Doing so will help you save money on the expensive fees these companies require. But if you have a lot to do and very little time to devote to the repair process yourself, a credit agency may be your best bet.

You Have the Law on Your Side.

There are laws to protect you from fraud and incorrect credit reporting (Federal Trade Commission, 2023)[45]. It may take some time to learn and understand these laws and how they can be applied in your specific situation, but in the long run, knowing these laws will undoubtedly help you improve your credit and also help you make an excellent case. It is also good "additional knowledge" that remains yours forever.

Credit Bureaus Will Listen to You.

Credit bureaus have thirty days to investigate any claims, whether made by a credit repair company or yourself (Federal Trade Commission, 2023)[45]. However, you must provide them with enough information, documentation, and evidence for them to make a decision.

WHY A CREDIT REPAIR AGENCY IS NOT THE ANSWER FOR MOST PEOPLE.

Are you considering contacting a credit repair company to clean up your bad credit report? You may need to rethink your decision to opt for an agency if you consider the following factors:

- You never get to solve the problem from the root.
- Chances are that some terrible money habits got you into the "mess" in the first place.
- Using shortcuts instead of unlearning these habits will inevitably set off a new debt cycle until you struggle to pay it off each month.
- A battered credit rating would definitely leave anyone disturbed, but fixing or having "credit fixers" delete accurate negative credit information from your report may leave a lasting belief that you have cheated the system (Consumer Financial Protection Bureau, 2023)[7]. Even if you get away

with it, it is usually only temporary. Just remember, no adverse reports can be deleted by any means.

- Once the credit bureau discovers your correct credit information, it will return to your reports. Yes, straight back to square one, and by that time, your "fixer" will be long gone and probably already forgot you even "happened."

Simply put, you cannot simply waltz out of missed payments and collection accounts just like that. A bad credit rating can only be fixed with time and money (Fair Isaac Corporation, 2025)[14]. Erasing accurate negative information on your credit report may seem like an intelligent move at first, but it will hurt you in the long run. Why not opt for the slow-and-steady approach instead of taking the "easy" route? If you have too many true negatives on your report, no "smart moves" from "smart experts" will fix that genuinely. Apply the recommended credit repair methods outlined in the chapter on fixing bad credit and watch your rating rebound slowly and—most importantly—steadily.

However, suppose you find incorrect information on your credit reports, such as a collection account that isn't yours or unfamiliar details listed as yours. In that case, you should file a dispute to correct it (Federal Trade Commission, 2023)[45]. Such mistakes happen all the time, which is just one more reason you should always check every credit report you receive for errors. No matter the state of your credit report, do not lose heart. More than a handful of creditors are willing to look beyond an old credit report as long as your recent history improves.

In conclusion, before you go on a spending or borrowing spree simply because you have access to credit, never forget that creditors are not in the business of helping you have those "amazing" credit card moments. They are in business because they have to make money. Do you really want to help them make money at your expense?

CHAPTER 9
SAVING FOR A HOME

"Start where you are. Use what you have. Do what you can."
Arthur Ashe

Becoming a homeowner is one of the most important life goals, but it's also not as simple as it sounds. Depending on where you want to live and your yearly income, buying a house can be highly challenging, and being selected for a mortgage has everything to do with not only credit approval but also the money you have to put down on your dream home.

Once you have your credit to a place where getting approved for a mortgage won't be an issue, the next thing you want to focus on is saving for a down payment for your home.

Here are six steps to saving for a home that will help you reach that goal sooner than later.

1. Set a goal

The first thing to do is set a goal. To plan the rest of the process, you have to know, at least to some degree, what type of housing you can and want to buy.

If you need some help at this point, try asking yourself these questions:

- Do I want a house, condo/townhome, or manufactured home?
- Where do I want to live?
- What type of services and amenities do I need nearby (including schools, grocery stores, malls, and parks)?
- When do I need to be able to move in?

- Am I willing to commute to work?

After doing this, you will have a more straightforward path toward the type of place you are looking for, and the rest of your to-do list will be a lot easier to narrow down.

2. Figure out how much you need

Now that you know what you want, it's time to adapt that desire into your reality. Adjust your home mortgage payment to 40% of your gross earnings to determine your maximum mortgage loan and purchase price (Bankrate, 2025)[27]. If you are not debt-free when buying, your mortgage payment may not be more than 25-30% of your gross income to keep your debt-to-income ratio below 45-50%.

The math is simple: Saving about 25 percent of your take-home income each month will allow you to create a downpayment on a home (Federal Reserve, 2024)[1]. The national average down payment and closing cost percentage is 7%.

Next, determine how much you can save in ten years. This should be near your house budget, so you hit an initial quote around the two-to-five-year period. For example, If you earn fifty thousand dollars a year after taxes, 25 percent will be twelve thousand, five hundred dollars a year in house savings.

To save that much, the next step will prove quite helpful.

3. Stop using your credit cards

Credit cards should not be used for living expenses. The best way to use credit is for emergencies. Even when that happens, you should have a plan to pay it off quickly and within a month.

The interest and fees paid for credit cards can comprise a significant part of your expenses every year, and by only using the money you have, you can move that money from your expenses to your savings (Consumer Financial Protection Bureau, 2023)[7]. So avoid using your credit cards as much as possible. As a rule of thumb, if you have to charge something on your credit card, you shouldn't be buying it.

4. Cut back on expenses

Do you know how much you spend every month/year on things that could be cut? Look at your monthly/yearly expenses and decide which can be cut. Besides avoiding the fees charged by credit cards and personal loans, you can save even more if you control your daily expenses.

5. Make a budget

Almost every professional advisor will tell you to make a budget. In business management, there is a saying: "What you don't measure, you can't control." This applies to managing your income as well.

Create a monthly budget in which you write down all necessary expenses and some leisure within acceptable terms, and ensure that you are leaving 25 percent of your income as savings for this specific goal.

A popular rule says that you should limit your basic expenses (the "needs") to 50 percent of your budget, leaving 30 percent for your "wants" and 20 percent for your savings (Federal Reserve, 2024)[1].

As for this point, when you put yourself in saving mode, the idea is to switch those last two figures and limit your "wants" to 20 percent of your income. Contributing 30 percent of your income toward savings and investments will boost you toward your new house.

6. Set up automatic savings

By this point, you should already know how much you save each month. But there are ways to boost your savings further.

A great way to go, of course, is to open an automatic savings account, which has the following benefits:

- If you are an employee, the designated percentage of your paycheck will go directly into your savings account, which will prevent you from the temptation of using it.

- If you work for yourself, you can link the savings account to your checking account and send part of the money automatically upon receiving the payments from your clients.

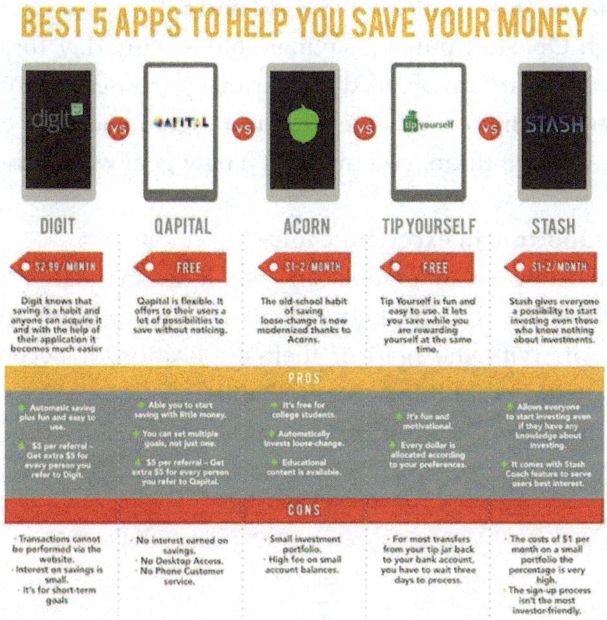

BEST 5 APPS TO HELP YOU SAVE MONEY

Here are the five most popular and useful apps available for Android and Apple users. They won't make you a millionaire overnight, but they will definitely set your mind on the right track and could help you move from non-saver to saver or debtor to investor.

1. Oportun (formally Digit)

Oportun is an app that tracks spending to determine how much is available for savings. A small amount of money is then withdrawn from your linked bank account and transferred to your Oportun account. The app's primary focus is automatically enabling users to save without noticing.

Those withdrawals are usually small—an average of $9 per transaction—to ensure users are comfortable with them. The amount could be higher or lower, depending on your spending history and bank account balance; it is usually between $2 and $30.

Although Oportun puts all savings into a rainy day fund, savings made with Oportun can be used for various purposes. You can choose what you are saving for. Whether that is a dream vacation, emergency fund, or IRA contribution, you must set a new goal within the Oportun app.

Why is Oportun an excellent choice?

Oportun believes that anyone can save. It doesn't matter how big or small your income is; Digit knows that saving is a habit and anyone can acquire it. With the help of their application, it becomes much easier to start and build this powerful habit.

How much does Oportun cost?

Oportun isn't a free app – you'll need to pay $5.00 per month to use it.

PROS:

- Automatic saving – fun and easy to use. You determine how much to save and navigate the process via simple text messaging. You can even choose not to make any transfers if you wish to do so.
- Simplified goals – A rainy day fund lets you determine only one small goal to work toward in the present, making saving simpler.
- $5 per referral – Earn an extra $5 for every person you introduce to Oportun. It's a reward for your trust in us and a motivation to share the benefits of our app with others.

CONS:

- It costs $5 per month.
- Transactions cannot be performed via the website.

- Interest on savings is small.
- It's best for short-term goals.

2. Qapital

Qapital offers users the ability to set savings goals and determine the best triggers for those goals. When a trigger is hit, a small amount of money – a predetermined amount – is transferred to your savings account from your bank account. This application is excellent for short-term savings goals. What's particularly interesting is that you can share your financial goals with others if you need encouragement to keep saving. Or you can choose to set up joint goals – in this case, you and those you choose will save together toward one particular goal.

Why is Qapital an excellent choice?

Qapital is flexible. It offers a lot of possibilities to save without noticing. Users can determine triggers they hit daily, such as liking blog posts or watching a video on YouTube, and a small amount of money will be transferred to savings without them even noticing.

How much does Qapital cost?

Qapital starts at $3/ month for their basic service

PROS:

- You can start saving with a small amount of money. You can set multiple goals, not just one.
- 30-day free trial.
- For each new friend you refer to Qapital, you'll receive $5.

CONS:

- No interest earned on savings.
- No desktop access.
- No phone customer service.
- Their premier plan is $12/month

3. Acorn

Thanks to Acorn, the old-school habit of saving loose change has been modernized. Your purchases will be automatically rounded up whenever you use your credit or debit card linked to an Acorn savings account. That small amount will be transferred to a special computer-managed investment portfolio.

Acorn offers two types of savings accounts, each with its own unique benefits. The first, a taxable investment account, is designed for regular users-particularly the younger generation keen to save some extra cash and develop a saving habit. This account, costing just $1 per month, empowers you to take control of your financial future.

The second, Acorns Later, is a retirement account that can help you save for your IRA. It costs $2 per month. Students get a special discount and an opportunity to use Acorn for free for four years while studying.

Why is Acorn an excellent choice?

Acorn is an excellent choice as it gives many options to save and determine how to allocate that loose change you've collected. You can set every penny to be transferred automatically into a savings account, or you can manually go through all purchases and then determine which rounds up to withdraw. Everything is flexible and easy to use.

How much does Acorn cost?

Acorn is free for college users. Taxable Acorn savings accounts cost $1 monthly, while Acorn Later costs $3 monthly.

PROS:

- Acorn is free for college students. It automatically invests the loose change.
- Educational content is available.

CONS:

- Small investment portfolio.
- High fee on small account balances.

4. Tip Yourself

Tip Yourself was made to make savings fun and easy. It lets you save by celebrating small everyday victories by tipping yourself. Small accomplishments now aren't just rewarded and allow you to raise a savings fund. Positivity differentiates this application from the rest of the micro-savings app field.

With Tip Yourself, every dollar you withdraw from your account can be allocated to your tip jar, based on your preferences. Setting up your tip jar goals is a breeze. Simply name your tip jars and set a specific amount you want to reach. It's that simple.

Why is Tip Yourself an excellent choice?

Tip Yourself is fun and easy to use. It lets you save while you are rewarding yourself at the same time. It's an excellent way to ensure you keep up with your everyday goals; it helps you stay on track and not forget how fulfilling it can be working on your goals from day to day.

How much does Tip Yourself cost?

Tip Yourself is a free application.

PROS:

- It's fun and motivational.
- You'll save to meet one of your goals while meeting other goals in your life.

CONS:

- You must wait three days for processing on most transfers from your tip jar back to your bank account.

5. Stash

Stash is designed to make investing more straightforward and more accessible. If you ever wanted to become an investor but found investor jargon too complicated or the barrier to entry too high, Stash allows you to overcome those obstacles. Stash lets you start investing with as little as $5. It also makes choosing investments extremely simple.

Stash also offers a Stash Retirement feature, a dedicated retirement account for investors. While Stash Retirement costs a dollar more than Stash Invest – [$2 per month], it's important to note that Stash Invest is only [$1 per month]. However, the real value of Stash is in its free trial period for the first three months. This unique feature allows you to start earning a return on your investment and potentially cover the monthly subscription cost, making it a smart choice for your retirement planning.

Why is Stash an excellent choice?

Stash is an excellent choice as it allows everyone to start investing —even those who know nothing about investments. It's quite a simple, intuitive app that makes an excellent starting point for new investors with little or no investing knowledge. It lowers the barriers to entry and helps you overcome the difficulties of investment jargon.

How much does Stash cost?

Stash offers two options: Stash Invest, which costs $3 per month, and Stash Retire, which costs $9.

PROS:

- Allows everyone to start investing even if they have no former investing knowledge.
- Investment guidance is excellent. The Stash Coach feature helps serve users' best interests.
- Low account minimum – only $5 is required to open an account.

CONS:

- The cost of $3-$9 per month is a very high percentage of a small portfolio.
- The sign-up process could be more investor-friendly.

HOW MUCH MORTGAGE CAN I AFFORD?

Ideally, your debt should only generate monthly payments of 45 percent of your income, including your mortgage (Bankrate, 2025)[27].

Consider this: if you earn eight thousand a month, you could aim to obtain a mortgage loan that, along with your consumer debt, does not exceed thirty-six hundred dollars a month. Your income and debt will ultimately determine your living situation. The more you earn and the less debt you have, the more houses you can buy and the better neighborhood you can live in. This potential for better housing options can be a powerful motivator to improve your financial status.

If you need to know how much you can afford, use The Power Is Now Mortgage Calculator to avoid going for a loan that creates a long-term financial problem.

CHAPTER 10
RESOURCES FOR CREDIT EMPOWERMENT

Credit, often seen as a numerical reflection of financial reliability, is today's cornerstone of stability and opportunity. Although crucial, the journey to establish credit can be complex and uncertain. However, armed with the right tools and knowledge, this path becomes both navigable and empowering.

In this section, we embark on an insightful journey, exploring the crucial resources for building a solid credit foundation. Here, we aim to present this often daunting subject with clarity and directness, ensuring that anyone, regardless of their financial background, can understand the mechanisms of credit without unnecessary jargon or confusion.

Understanding the vital role that credit plays in our lives, we will address the significance of credit history beyond mere numerical representation. We will unravel the tools, strategies, and resources that serve as the building blocks for a robust credit profile (Fair Isaac Corporation, 2025)[14].

The goal is to offer information and provide an engaging roadmap encouraging comprehension and action. Credit establishment is not just about data; it's a significant part of one's financial journey, shaping opportunities and framing financial stability. Join us in this exploration as we uncover the tools and insights that can assist in creating a sound financial footing, enabling you to wield the power of credit to its fullest potential, transforming your financial life.

"Establishing good credit involves a mix of resources and strategic actions that collectively contribute to a favorable credit profile. To establish good credit, individuals can leverage various resources and strategies."

HERE ARE SOME ESSENTIAL RESOURCES:

1. Secured Credit Cards:

These cards require a deposit that serves as collateral. They are an excellent tool for building credit as they report to credit bureaus, helping individuals establish a positive credit history (Consumer Financial Protection Bureau, 2023)[7].

2. Credit Builder Loans:

These help individuals build credit. Borrowers make fixed payments into a savings account or CD, and once the loan is repaid, they receive the money plus the interest earned. This activity gets reported to credit bureaus, reflecting responsible payment behavior (Consumer Financial Protection Bureau, 2023)[7].

3. Authorized User Status:

Being added as an authorized user on someone else's credit card account, especially that of a family member or a close friend with a good credit history, can help establish a credit history (Fair Isaac Corporation, 2025)[14]. As an authorized user, the primary account holder's positive credit behavior reflects on the user's credit report.

4. Credit Counseling Services:

Non-profit credit counseling organizations can guide managing credit, debt, and budgeting (Consumer Financial Protection Bureau, 2023)[7]. They offer educational resources and may assist in disputing inaccuracies on credit reports.

5. Credit Monitoring Services:

Subscribing to a credit monitoring service can help individuals stay updated on changes to their credit reports (MyFICO, 2025)[26]. These services often provide alerts for potential identity theft and assist in maintaining a vigilant eye on credit activities.

6. Financial Education Resources:

Numerous online platforms, community courses, and even some banks offer financial literacy and education resources (Federal Reserve, 2024)[1]. These materials can educate individuals on the importance of credit, how to manage it, and how to make wise financial decisions.

7. Debt Repayment Strategies:

Understanding and implementing effective debt repayment strategies can positively impact credit scores (Bankrate, 2025)[27]. By reducing outstanding debts and making regular, timely payments, individuals can steadily improve their credit standing.

8. Rental Reporting Services:

Some services allow rental payment data to be reported to credit bureaus, helping individuals with limited credit history build a favorable credit profile based on their on-time rent payments (Consumer Financial Protection Bureau, 2023)[7].

9. Employer Assistance Programs:

Certain employers offer programs to help employees build credit, offering financial wellness initiatives or partnerships with financial institutions for credit-building products (Federal Reserve, 2024)[1].

By leveraging these diverse resources and implementing effective strategies, individuals can proactively take steps toward establishing and enhancing their credit profiles. Consistent and responsible use of these tools contributes to a more robust financial foundation and opens doors to future economic opportunities.

Let's break each resource down for you:

1. SECURED CREDIT CARDS

Secured credit cards are a type of credit card that requires a cash deposit as collateral. They are designed for individuals establishing credit for the first time, trying to rebuild their credit, or having a limited credit history (Consumer Financial Protection Bureau, 2023)[7]. The deposit made by the cardholder typically determines their credit limit.

Key features of secured credit cards include:

Collateral Requirement: To obtain a secured credit card, the cardholder must deposit cash with the issuing bank. This deposit acts as collateral and protects the card issuer if the cardholder fails to make payments.

Credit Limit: The credit limit on a secured credit card is usually equivalent to a percentage of the cash deposit. For instance, if a cardholder deposits $500, their credit limit will likely be around $500. Depending on the card issuer's policies, this limit may be slightly higher or lower.

Credit Building: Secured credit cards are a powerful tool for building or rebuilding credit (Fair Isaac Corporation, 2025)[14]. By using the card responsibly—making timely payments and keeping credit utilization low—individuals can establish a positive credit history. The regular reporting of activity to credit bureaus contributes to the gradual, but hopeful, improvement of the cardholder's credit score.

Usage Similar to Unsecured Cards: Secured credit cards offer the same level of flexibility as traditional unsecured credit cards. They can be used for making purchases, paying bills, and accessing credit in the same way. Cardholders receive monthly statements and have the control to make minimum payments on their balances.

Possibility of Transitioning to Unsecured Card: Some secured credit card issuers periodically review cardholders' credit histories (Consumer Financial Protection Bureau, 2023)[7]. With a demonstrated pattern of responsible credit usage and on-time payments, they may offer the option to transition to an unsecured credit card. This often involves returning the initial deposit to the cardholder.

Secured credit cards provide a pathway for individuals with limited or damaged credit to demonstrate responsible credit behavior. By using these cards wisely and responsibly, cardholders can build a positive credit history, ultimately improving their overall credit standing and increasing their eligibility for traditional credit products (Fair Isaac Corporation, 2025)[14].

Here are some well-known companies that historically offered secured credit cards:

- Capital One: Capital One is a major credit card issuer known to offer secured credit cards.
- Discover: Discover is another major credit card issuer that often providing secured credit cards.
- Bank of America: Bank of America is a well-established bank that may offer secured credit card options.
- Wells Fargo: Wells Fargo is a financial institution that has previously offered secured credit cards.
- CitiBank: Citibank is a global bank that may have options for secured credit cards.
- U.S. Bank: U.S. Bank is another financial institution that has historically offered secured credit cards.
- OpenSky: OpenSky is a financial services company specializing in secured credit cards.
- First Progress: First Progress is known for providing secured credit cards that focus on helping individuals build or rebuild credit.
- Applied Bank: Applied Bank is a financial institution that may offer secured credit card options.
- Green Dot Bank: Green Dot is known for its prepaid cards and may offer secured credit cards.

2. CREDIT BUILDER LOANS

Credit builder loans are financial products designed to help individuals establish or improve their credit scores (Consumer Financial Protection Bureau, 2023)[7]. These loans are structured uniquely to assist borrowers in building a positive credit history.

Here's how credit builder loans typically work:

Structure: When an individual takes out a credit builder loan, the borrowed money is not immediately disbursed to the borrower. Instead, the lending institution holds the loan amount in a savings account or certificate of deposit (CD).

Repayment Plan: The borrower makes fixed monthly payments toward the loan, usually over a fixed term, such as six months or a year. These payments are reported to the credit bureaus (Consumer Financial Protection Bureau, 2023)[7].

Delayed Access to Funds: In contrast to traditional loans, the borrower does not receive the loan amount until the loan term ends and all payments have been made. This unique feature of credit builder loans ensures a disciplined approach to credit building. At the loan's completion, the lender releases the total amount (minus any fees or interest charges) to the borrower.

Positive credit Impact: Each on-time payment made by the borrower on the credit builder loan is reported to the major credit bureaus (Fair Isaac Corporation, 2025)[14]. These regular and punctual payments demonstrate responsible credit behavior, significantly contributing to the establishment of a positive credit history.

Interest and Fees: Credit builder loans might have interest charges or administrative fees. However, some lenders offer credit builder loans with no interest or fees, aiming primarily to assist individuals in building credit.

Credit builder loans are particularly beneficial for individuals with no credit history or who are working to repair damaged credit (Consumer Financial Protection Bureau, 2023)[7]. By regularly making loan payments, borrowers can establish a track record of on-time payments, improving their credit scores.

Once the loan term is complete and all payments have been made, the borrower receives the total loan amount. This helps in building savings while simultaneously improving the individual's credit profile.

These loans are an excellent option for those who may not qualify for traditional loans due to a lack of credit history or a low credit score. By using credit builder loans wisely, individuals can lay a foundation for a more substantial credit history and pave the way for future financial opportunities.

Here are some of the companies that offer Credit Builder Loans.

If you have a limited credit history or derogatory credit, some companies offer financial products designed to accommodate individuals in such situations. Remember that the availability of specific products can change, and it's crucial to review the terms and conditions of each offering. As of the time of writing this book, here are some companies that may be more lenient regarding credit history:

- Self (formerly Self Lender): Self offers a Credit Builder Account, a combination of a small loan and a forced savings plan. Payments are reported to the credit bureaus, helping to build credit.
- Credit Strong: Credit Strong provides credit builder loans with terms ranging from 12 to 24 months. These loans help individuals build credit history through installment loans.
- Chime Credit Builder Visa Secured Credit Card: Chime offers a credit builder program that combines a secured credit card with a credit builder feature.
- Esusu: Esusu provides a Credit Builder Loan that allows users to build credit by making small monthly payments reported to the credit bureaus.
- LendUp: LendUp offers credit builder loans as part of its mission to provide credit access for individuals with limited credit history.
- Navy Federal Credit Union: Navy Federal Credit Union provides credit builder loans to its members, helping them establish or rebuild credit.
- OneMain Financial: OneMain Financial offers personal loans, including credit builder loans, to help individuals build credit over time.
- First Tech Federal Credit Union: This Credit Union provides credit builder loans to its members, allowing them to establish or improve their credit.
- Digital Federal Credit Union (DCU): DCU offers a credit builder loan to help members build or rebuild their credit history.
- TD Bank's Right Step Program: TD Bank offers a Right Step Program that includes a credit builder loan to assist individuals in establishing or improving credit.

Before applying for any credit product, it's essential to carefully review the terms, fees, and conditions associated with the specific offering. Also, remember that the credit industry is dynamic, and new products may be introduced while existing ones may change. Always check the latest information on the issuer's website or contact them directly for the most up-to-date details.

3. AUTHORIZED USER STATUS

Authorized user status refers to a credit arrangement where an individual is granted permission to use someone else's credit account (Fair Isaac Corporation, 2025)[14]. Typically, the primary account holder (the credit account owner) can add another person as an authorized user, allowing them to make purchases using the primary account holder's credit card.

Key points about authorized user status:

Credit Card Access: Once added as an authorized user, the individual gains the power to manage a credit card linked to the primary account holder's credit account. This card can be used to make purchases, giving the authorized user a sense of financial control.

Credit Reporting: Positive or negative credit activity made by the authorized user can be reported on their credit report based on the credit card issuer's policies (Consumer Financial Protection Bureau, 2023)[7]. The account history, including payment history and credit utilization, typically gets reported to the credit bureaus for both the primary account holder and the authorized user.

Responsibilities: While authorized users are not legally responsible for repaying debts incurred on the credit card, it's important to note that the primary account holder and the authorized user share a responsibility. The primary account holder retains full responsibility for the charges made by the authorized user, but it's a shared financial journey.

Impact on Credit: The primary account holder's responsible credit behavior positively influences the authorized user's credit history (Fair Isaac Corporation, 2025)[14]. Regular and timely payments on the account build a favorable credit profile for the authorized user.

However, missed payments or high credit utilization can also negatively affect the authorized user's credit.

Limitations: While authorized user status can be beneficial for building credit, it may sometimes carry a different weight than having an individual's independent credit history. Lenders and credit institutions may consider this a less influential factor in determining creditworthiness than having one's credit accounts and history.

Authorized user status is often used by parents adding their children to their credit cards to help them establish credit or by individuals looking to benefit from a family member's or friend's good credit history. It's a way to share the advantages of a positive credit history with others and assist them in building or improving their credit.

Being added as an authorized user on someone else's credit card can be a pathway to growth and improvement in your credit history. However, it's important to note that not all credit card issuers report authorized user activity to credit bureaus (Consumer Financial Protection Bureau, 2023)[7]. Here are some companies that have a track record of facilitating authorized user status:

Here are some companies that facilitate Authorized User Status:

- American Express: American Express has been known to report authorized user activity to credit bureaus. Being added as an authorized user on an American Express card may contribute to your credit history.
- Chase: Chase is another major credit card issuer that generally reports authorized user activity to credit bureaus. Being added to a Chase credit card could impact your credit history.
- CitiBank: CitiBank has been known to report authorized user activity to credit bureaus. Being added as an authorized user on a Citi credit card may affect your credit history.
- Discover: Discover is known to report authorized user activity to credit bureaus. Being added as an authorized user on a Discover card could help you build credit.
- Capital One: Capital One has historically reported

authorized user activity to credit bureaus. Being added to a Capital One credit card might impact your credit history.

- Bank of America: Bank of America generally reports authorized user activity to credit bureaus. Being added as an authorized user on a Bank of America credit card may contribute to your credit history.
- Barclays: Barclays is another credit card issuer known to report authorized user activity to credit bureaus.
- Wells Fargo: Wells Fargo may report authorized user activity to credit bureaus. Being added as an authorized user on a Wells Fargo credit card could impact your credit history.

Remember that these companies' credit reporting practices may change, so verifying the current policies by contacting the specific credit card issuer is essential. Additionally, not all credit card issuers report authorized user activity, so check with the issuer before assuming that being added as an authorized user will positively impact your credit history.

4. CREDIT COUNSELING SERVICES

Managing credit and debt can become daunting in a world of financial complexities. Enter credit counseling services—a beacon of guidance in fiscal uncertainty. Often, non-profit organizations stand as pillars of support, offering education, advice, and strategies to navigate the labyrinth of personal finances (Consumer Financial Protection Bureau, 2023)[7].

Understanding Credit Counseling Services

Credit counseling services provide individuals with the tools and knowledge to make informed financial decisions. They offer guidance on budgeting, debt management, credit improvement, and financial planning through one-on-one sessions, workshops, and online resources.

Services Offered

Financial Evaluation: Credit counseling services typically begin by evaluating an individual's financial situation. They assess income, expenses, debts, and credit reports to understand the economic landscape (Consumer Financial Protection Bureau, 2023)[7].

Budgeting Assistance: They help create and manage realistic budgets, offering strategies to control spending and save for financial goals.

Debt Management Plans: Credit counseling services often develop debt management plans for those struggling. These plans involve negotiating with creditors to create more manageable repayment schedules (Consumer Financial Protection Bureau, 2023)[7].

Credit Improvement Guidance: They offer advice on improving credit scores, emphasizing factors such as payment history, credit utilization, and building a positive credit history (Fair Isaac Corporation, 2025)[14].

Financial Education: Workshops, seminars, and online resources are provided to educate individuals on various economic topics, including credit, saving, and investment (Federal Reserve, 2024)[1].

The Role in Credit Repair

Credit counseling services play a crucial role in helping individuals repair their credit. They offer strategies to manage and reduce debt, improve credit behaviors, and create sustainable financial habits, paving the way toward a healthier credit profile (Consumer Financial Protection Bureau, 2023)[7].

Counseling Process

The process often involves an initial consultation, during which financial experts assess the individual's situation. From there, a personalized plan is developed, focusing on areas that need improvement. Regular follow-ups and check-ins help ensure progress and offer ongoing support.

Benefits of Credit Counseling Services:

Professional Guidance: Trained financial counselors provide tailored advice based on individual financial situations.

Debt Relief: Assistance in negotiating with creditors can lead to reduced interest rates or more manageable repayment terms (Consumer Financial Protection Bureau, 2023)[7].

Education and Empowerment: Individuals become empowered to make sound financial decisions independently through education (Federal Reserve, 2024)[1].

Credit counseling services serve as guiding lights in the often turbulent waters of personal finance. They offer education, support, and practical strategies to help individuals navigate their way to financial stability and credit wellness. By fostering responsible financial habits, these services empower individuals to take control of their economic destinies and pave the way toward a more secure future.

Specialized agencies often provide credit counseling and repair services that aim to assist individuals in managing their debt and improving their credit scores. It's important to note that while credit counseling focuses on budgeting, debt management, and financial education, credit repair services often involve working to remove inaccuracies or errors from credit reports (Consumer Financial Protection Bureau, 2023)[7]. Always exercise caution and thoroughly research any company offering credit-related services. As of my last update in January 2022, here are some companies that have been known for providing credit counseling and credit repair services:

Here are some of the companies that offer credit counseling and repair services:

- National Foundation for Credit Counseling (NFCC): NFCC is a non-profit organization that provides credit counseling services and financial education.
- Money Management International (MMI): MMI is a non-profit credit counseling agency that offers services to help individuals manage debt and improve their financial situation.

- GreenPath Financial Wellness: GreenPath is a non-profit organization that provides credit counseling, debt management, and financial education services.
- Consumer Credit Counseling Service (CCCS): CCCS agencies, often affiliated with the NFCC, offer credit counseling services to help individuals with debt management.

Credit Repair Services:

- Lexington Law: Lexington Law is a credit repair firm that works to challenge and dispute items on credit reports that may be inaccurate, outdated, or unverifiable.
- CreditRepair.com: CreditRepair.com offers credit repair services, including credit monitoring and personalized credit improvement plans.
- Sky Blue Credit Repair: Sky Blue Credit Repair focuses on credit repair services, helping individuals address inaccuracies and improve their credit reports.
- Ovation Credit Services: Ovation Credit Services provides credit repair solutions, including personalized credit dispute strategies.
- The Credit People: The Credit People offer credit repair services focusing on affordability and personalized credit improvement plans.

Always be cautious when considering credit repair services as legitimate concerns and regulations surrounding this industry (Federal Trade Commission, 2023)[45]. It's advisable to check reviews, verify the company's reputation with the Better Business Bureau, and be aware of any fees associated with the services. Additionally, remember that no company can guarantee specific results regarding credit score improvement, as individual credit histories vary. Consulting with a certified financial counselor or advisor may also be worthwhile if you seek assistance with credit-related issues.

5. CREDIT MONITORING SERVICES

Credit monitoring services are designed to help individuals monitor changes in their credit reports from major credit bureaus (Consumer Financial Protection Bureau, 2023)[7]. These services offer ongoing monitoring and alerts related to activities that can affect an individual's credit standing.

Continuous Monitoring: Credit monitoring services track credit reports from major credit bureaus (Equifax, Experian, and TransUnion) for any changes. They regularly check for updates, including new accounts opened, credit inquiries, changes in personal information, and reported payments.

Alerts and Notifications: These services alert subscribers whenever significant changes occur in their credit reports (MyFICO, 2025)[26]. For instance, an alert may be sent if a new credit account is opened in the individual's name or there's a significant change in their credit score. Notifications can help individuals quickly respond to any potentially fraudulent or unauthorized activities.

Identity Theft Protection: Credit monitoring services often include identity theft protection features. These features monitor for signs of identity theft, such as unauthorized use of personal information, and alert the subscriber to suspicious activities (MyFICO, 2025)[26].

Access to Credit Scores: Some credit monitoring services offer access to credit scores, providing regular updates on an individual's credit standing (MyFICO, 2025)[26]. This allows subscribers to keep track of their progress and understand how their financial behaviors affect their credit.

Credit Report Analysis: These services may offer tools to help subscribers understand the information in their credit reports. They might explain specific terms or elements of the report and offer advice on improving credit health (Consumer Financial Protection Bureau, 2023)[7].

Purpose and Benefits: Credit monitoring services aim to help individuals detect and prevent identity theft and fraud. By receiving timely alerts about any suspicious activity on their credit reports, subscribers can take immediate action to rectify issues and protect their credit.

Cost and Availability: Credit monitoring services are available from various providers and often have a subscription fee. Some financial institutions, credit card companies, or identity protection firms may offer these services for free or as part of a broader package of financial products.

In a world where identity theft and fraud are prevalent, credit monitoring services provide an extra layer of protection. They provide individuals with the tools to stay informed and vigilant about their credit health. Being aware of changes in credit reports allows subscribers to take swift action in case of discrepancies or potential fraudulent activities, thereby safeguarding their financial well-being (MyFICO, 2025)[26].

Here are some companies that offer credit monitoring services:

Credit monitoring services help individuals monitor changes to their credit reports and detect potential identity theft or fraudulent activities. Many companies offer credit monitoring services, and they may vary in terms of features, pricing, and additional offerings.

- Credit Karma: Credit Karma offers free credit monitoring services and provides access to credit scores and credit reports from Equifax and TransUnion.
- Credit Sesame: Credit Sesame provides free credit monitoring services and tools to help users improve their credit.
- IdentityForce: IdentityForce offers comprehensive identity theft protection, including credit monitoring services, dark web monitoring, and more.
- myFICO: myFICO, a division of Fair Isaac Corporation, provides credit monitoring services and access to FICO scores and credit reports.
- Experian: Experian, one of the major credit bureaus, offers

credit monitoring services through its identity protection products.

- TransUnion: Another central credit bureau, TransUnion, offers credit monitoring services through various products.
- Equifax: Equifax, one of the three major credit bureaus, offers credit monitoring services through its identity protection and credit monitoring products.
- LifeLock: LifeLock, now part of Norton 360, offers identity theft protection services, including credit monitoring.
- PrivacyGuard: PrivacyGuard provides credit monitoring services, identity theft protection, and credit reports from all three major credit bureaus.
- Identity Guard: Identity Guard offers credit monitoring services, identity theft protection, and dark web monitoring.
- CreditWise by Capital One: CreditWise is a free credit monitoring service provided by Capital One, offering credit reports and monitoring from TransUnion.
- Credit.com: Credit.com provides free credit monitoring services, credit reports, and educational resources to help users understand and improve their credit.

Please note that the credit monitoring industry is dynamic, and new services may be introduced while existing services may change. Always check the latest information on the respective company's website or contact them directly for the most up-to-date details on features, pricing, and terms. Additionally, it's crucial to review the terms and conditions of any credit monitoring service to ensure it meets your specific needs and preferences.

6. FINANCIAL EDUCATION RESOURCES

Financial education resources encompass various materials, tools, and programs to enhance individuals' knowledge and understanding of economic concepts (Federal Reserve, 2024)[1]. These resources aim to empower people with the necessary information and skills to make informed financial decisions.

Types of Financial Education Resources

Online Courses and Webinars: Numerous websites and online platforms offer free or paid courses covering diverse financial topics. These resources include video tutorials, interactive modules, and webinars on budgeting, investing, managing debt, understanding credit, and more (Federal Reserve, 2024)[1].

Blogs and Articles: Financial blogs and articles provide valuable insights into personal finance matters. Financial experts often write these, offering practical tips, advice, and explanations on various economic topics (Bankrate, 2025)[27].

Books and Publications: Many books covering personal finance, investment strategies, budgeting, and wealth management are available. These resources cater to different levels of financial literacy and provide in-depth knowledge on specific subjects.

Podcasts: Audio-based content discussing financial topics in an easily digestible format. Podcasts often feature interviews with experts and discussions on real-life financial scenarios, making the content relatable and engaging.

Apps and Tools: Numerous mobile and online applications are designed to assist with budgeting, expense tracking, investment management, and credit score monitoring. These resources make it easier for individuals to manage their finances daily.

Community Courses and Workshops: Local community centers, libraries, and educational institutions often host in-person workshops and courses covering financial literacy (Federal Reserve, 2024)[1]. These sessions may cover budgeting, saving, understanding credit, and retirement planning.

Importance of Financial Education Resources:

Empowerment: These resources aim to equip individuals with the knowledge and skills to control their financial lives. Understanding personal finance empowers people to make better financial decisions.

Decision Making: With a strong understanding of financial concepts, individuals can make more informed decisions about managing their money, investing, planning for the future, and avoiding debt (Federal Reserve, 2024)[1].

Long-Term Financial Health: Learning about budgeting, saving, and investing assists individuals in building a more secure financial future by creating good financial habits.

Avoiding Financial Pitfalls: Financial education helps individuals recognize potential risks and avoid common financial pitfalls, such as high-interest debt, overspending, and falling victim to scams (Consumer Financial Protection Bureau, 2023)[7].

Access to various educational resources is crucial in an increasingly complex financial landscape. These materials cater to different learning styles and levels of financial literacy, offering valuable information and practical advice to help individuals manage their finances.

7. DEBT REPAYMENT STRATEGIES

Debt repayment strategies are structured plans to help individuals efficiently pay off their debts, manage their financial obligations, and ultimately achieve a debt-free status (Bankrate, 2025)[27]. These strategies provide a roadmap for managing debt systematically and can vary based on an individual's economic situation and the debts they owe.

Here are some effective debt repayment strategies:

Debt Snowball Method: This method involves paying off the smallest debt first while making minimum payments on other debts. Once the smallest debt is cleared, the amount paid is directed toward the next smallest debt. The process continues, creating a "snowball effect" as each debt is paid off (Bankrate, 2025)[27].

Debt Avalanche Method: This approach tackles debts based on their interest rates. The focus is on paying off the debt with the highest interest rate first while making minimum payments on other debts. Once the highest-interest debt is cleared, the strategy continues with the debt having the next highest interest rate (Bankrate, 2025)[27].

Debt Consolidation: This strategy involves merging multiple debts into a single loan or credit account with a lower interest rate. Consolidation can simplify payments and reduce the overall interest paid, making it easier to manage debts (Consumer Financial Protection Bureau, 2023)[7].

Balance Transfer: For those with high-interest credit card debt, transferring balances to a new credit card with a lower introductory or promotional interest rate can save money on interest payments and facilitate quicker debt repayment.

Increasing Payments: Regardless of the specific strategy used, increasing the amount paid towards monthly debts accelerates the repayment process. Even a slight increase in payments beyond the minimum requirement can significantly reduce the time and interest paid on debts (Bankrate, 2025)[27].

Negotiating with Creditors: Communication with creditors to renegotiate terms, lower interest rates, or establish a more manageable payment plan can be a powerful debt management strategy, especially for those facing financial hardship (Consumer Financial Protection Bureau, 2023)[7].

Prioritizing High-Interest Debt: Focusing on debts with higher interest rates can save money in the long run. By paying off these high-interest debts first, individuals can reduce the total interest paid over time (Bankrate, 2025)[27].

Debt repayment strategies should be chosen based on individual circumstances, such as the amount and types of debts, available resources, and financial goals. What's crucial is selecting a strategy that fits one's economic situation and commitment to reduce debt while avoiding accruing additional debt effectively.

Commitment, discipline, and consistency are key in any debt repayment strategy. Choosing and sticking to a plan that aligns with one's financial situation can lead to a more successful journey toward becoming debt-free.

8. RENTAL REPORTING SERVICES

Rental reporting services allow individuals to have their rental payment history reported to credit bureaus (Consumer Financial Protection Bureau, 2023)[7]. Traditionally, rental payments do not automatically appear on credit reports, unlike mortgage payments or credit card balances. However, rental reporting services offer a way to include rental payment data in credit reports, potentially benefiting individuals seeking to build or improve their credit history.

Key points about rental reporting services:

Inclusion of Rental Payments on Credit Reports: These services work by reporting an individual's monthly rental payments to major credit bureaus, such as Equifax, Experian, or TransUnion (Consumer Financial Protection Bureau, 2023)[7]. Once reported, this data becomes a part of the individual's credit history.

Positive Impact on Credit History: Regular and on-time rental payments can positively impact an individual's credit history by demonstrating responsible financial behavior (Fair Isaac Corporation, 2025)[14]. This can be especially beneficial for those with limited credit history or those looking to strengthen their credit profile.

Participation by Landlords or Property Management Companies: Landlords or property management companies may need to enroll in rental reporting services to ensure the payment data gets reported to credit bureaus. Some platforms work directly with property managers or landlords to facilitate this process.

Voluntary Participation: Rental reporting services are typically voluntary for tenants and landlords. Tenants must agree to have their rental payments reported, and landlords or property managers must opt into the service to ensure accurate reporting.

Availability of Rental Reporting Platforms: Several third-party companies or platforms specialize in rental reporting services. They offer tenants a way to have their rental payment history reported to credit bureaus.

Impact on Credit Scores: While a positive rental payment history can improve credit scores, late or missed rental payments may negatively affect credit scores as late payments on loans or credit cards do (Fair Isaac Corporation, 2025)[14].

Building Credit for Renters: For those who primarily rent and do not have many traditional credit accounts, having their rental payment history reflected on their credit reports can be a way to build credit based on consistent financial responsibility.

Rental reporting services allow individuals to strengthen their credit profiles by incorporating regular, on-time rental payments into their credit history. This resource can be valuable, particularly for renters with limited credit reporting opportunities through traditional credit accounts (Consumer Financial Protection Bureau, 2023)[7].

Here are some of the companies that offer rental reporting services

Rental reporting services allow individuals to have their rental payment history reported to credit bureaus, which can be beneficial for building or improving credit scores.

- RentTrack: RentTrack allows tenants to report their rental payments to major credit bureaus to build credit history.
- LevelCredit: LevelCredit offers a service that reports rent payments to credit bureaus, contributing to the tenant's credit history.
- Esusu: Esusu is a platform that allows renters to report their rental payments to credit bureaus to impact their credit profiles positively.
- Rental Kharma: Rental Kharma enables tenants to report their rental payments to credit bureaus, potentially improving their credit scores.
- ClearNow: ClearNow is primarily a rent collection service, but it also allows tenants to have their rent payments reported to Experian RentBureau.
- PayYourRent: PayYourRent provides online rent payment services and allows tenants to report their rent payments to credit bureaus.
- Rock the Score: Rock the Score is a platform that allows renters to report their monthly rent payments to credit bureaus.
- RentalHistoryReports: RentalHistoryReports, a service by

CoreLogic, provides rental payment history reporting to credit bureaus.
- RentReporters: RentReporters allows tenants to report their rental payments to TransUnion and Equifax, potentially helping them build credit.
- Build (formerly known as Cozy): Build offers a service that allows tenants to report their rent payments to Experian RentBureau.
- Rentalutions: Rentalutions is primarily a property management platform, but it also allows tenants to have their rent payments reported to credit bureaus.

9. EMPLOYER ASSISTANCE PROGRAMS

Employer Assistance Programs, particularly financial wellness programs, are initiatives companies provide to support their employees in managing their finances, achieving greater financial literacy, and improving their overall well-being (Federal Reserve, 2024)[1]. These programs aim to alleviate financial stress and promote a more financially secure workforce.

Key elements of Employer Assistance Programs for financial wellness:

Financial Education and Workshops: Employers often offer workshops, seminars, or educational sessions covering various financial topics (Federal Reserve, 2024)[1]. These sessions may include budgeting, saving, investing, retirement planning, managing debt, and understanding credit.

Access to Financial Advisors: Some programs provide access to financial advisors or counselors who can offer personalized guidance to employees. These professionals assist individuals in setting financial goals, managing debt, and making informed financial decisions (Federal Reserve, 2024)[1].

Assistance with Retirement Plans: Employers may provide guidance and resources for employees to understand and make the most of their company-sponsored retirement plans, such as 401(k)s or pension schemes.

Employee Benefits and Resources: Companies often offer additional benefits contributing to employees' financial wellness, such as flexible spending accounts, health savings accounts, employee stock purchase plans, and financial planning tools (Federal Reserve, 2024)[1].

Financial Wellness Tools and Apps: Some employers provide access to financial wellness apps or online tools that help employees manage their money, track expenses, budget effectively, and monitor their credit.

Credit-Building Products: Certain programs might offer credit-building products or partnerships with financial institutions to help employees establish or improve their credit (Consumer Financial Protection Bureau, 2023)[7]. This may include access to credit-builder loans or secured credit cards.

Debt Management Assistance: Assistance programs may include resources or counseling to help employees effectively manage and pay off debts and offer strategies to reduce financial stress (Federal Reserve, 2024)[1].

Work-life balance and Financial Wellness Integration: Employers often recognize the link between financial stress and work performance. They may integrate financial wellness programs with work-life balance initiatives, mental health support, and stress management programs to ensure holistic employee well-being.

Employer-Matched Savings Programs: Some companies offer matching contributions to employees' savings or investment accounts, incentivizing them to save for the future (Federal Reserve, 2024)[1].

Employer Assistance Programs for financial wellness aim to create a supportive environment where employees can access resources and guidance to manage their finances more effectively. These programs recognize the importance of addressing financial stress in the workplace and how it can impact overall employee well-being and productivity.

In today's ever-evolving financial landscape, access to a myriad of resources is vital in navigating the complexities of personal finance. From credit building to debt management, financial education, and employer-provided assistance programs, these resources collectively serve as guidance and support, empowering individuals to make informed decisions and secure their economic well-being (Federal Reserve, 2024)[1].

As we traverse the realm of financial wellness, the availability of tools such as secured credit cards, credit builder loans, and rental reporting services offers pathways for individuals to establish and strengthen their credit profiles (Consumer Financial Protection Bureau, 2023)[7]. Meanwhile, debt repayment strategies like the debt snowball or avalanche methods pave the way toward financial freedom, aiding in systematically eradicating debt burdens (Bankrate, 2025)[27].

Financial education resources, whether through online courses, podcasts, or community workshops, act as the bedrock of knowledge, equipping individuals with the essential understanding to navigate the nuances of personal finance (Federal Reserve, 2024)[1]. These educational materials foster an environment of empowerment, allowing individuals to make informed decisions, manage their expenses, and invest wisely.

Employer assistance programs, particularly those focused on financial wellness, are pillars of support within the corporate landscape. These initiatives alleviate economic stress and nurture a more secure and productive workforce, intertwining employees' well-being with the organization's success (Federal Reserve, 2024)[1].

Ultimately, these diverse resources collectively provide a spectrum of tools and support, catering to individuals at various stages of their financial journeys. Whether establishing credit, managing debt, or gaining comprehensive financial literacy, these resources form an interconnected web, offering avenues for growth, stability, and a brighter economic future. By diligently applying these resources, individuals can carve a path toward financial independence, making sound decisions that lay the foundation for enduring stability and prosperity.

CHAPTER 11
CLIENT CASE STUDIES

I work with clients daily with credit challenges that they have never addressed but now want to be approved for a Home Loan. Their credit is the primary roadblock preventing them from getting approved for a home loan. They can no longer ignore the problem if they're going to succeed in getting a pre-approved home loan to be able to purchase their first home. My goal in every client meeting is to educate and identify the credit issues that have the most significant impact on their score and provide several strategies to increase their score (Fair Isaac Corporation, 2025)[14]. Below are five case studies of actual individuals and families. Their names have been changed to protect their identity.

CASE STUDY #1

Client: Mr. and Mrs. Taylor

Issue: Bad Credit: 520 + 600 Score

Mr. and Mrs. Taylor called me because they were tired of renting and wanted to buy a home to retire. I was very excited for them and ready to help them realize their home ownership dreams, but when I ran their credit report, the excitement turned to concern. I found that

Mrs. Taylor's credit score was 520, and Mr. Taylor's credit score was 600. Their low credit scores and high debt-to-income ratio prevented them from being approved for a loan (Fair Isaac Corporation, 2025)[14].

The only good news was that there are programs that allowed FICO scores as low as 620 (MyFICO, 2025)[26]. So, if I could help the Taylors raise their credit scores to 620, We could at least meet the minimum credit score requirement.

The Taylors had one credit card at the limit with a balance of $3,000. I advised them to pay off the credit card's entire balance as soon as possible. They did just that, taking Mr. Taylor's credit score from 600 to 621—a jump of twenty-one points. That increase in their credit score positions him to qualify for a home mortgage, but he would not be able to do so independently. He would also need Mrs. Taylor's score to improve to 620 because we needed both incomes to qualify.

Although Mr. Taylor had a low credit score, he didn't have a lot of debt. By paying off his credit card with the highest balance, he raised his credit score to qualify for a loan (Fair Isaac Corporation, 2025)[14]. Ms. Taylor still needed to improve her credit score and did not possess any significant credit beyond a single credit card with a limit of $1200 and a debt of $1,200. She was making minimum payments only, which barely covered the interest rate. Thus, the next step with Ms. Taylor was to pay at least half of her credit card off and apply for a secured credit card with the lowest possible APR and annual fee (Consumer Financial Protection Bureau, 2023)[7]. Mr. Taylor should've used half the money to pay down his credit card, which is Taylor's credit card. But instead, he paid off his credit card, and it took them an additional two months to pay off her credit card.

I advise the Taylors to establish additional credit solely to build credit and not increase dead. The Taylors got approved for a Mastercard credit card with a reasonably low APR. The card does not offer any incentives, such as points or bonuses, so there would not be as much of a temptation to use it often. A few months later, Ms. Taylor's credit score increased from 580 to 620, and her husband's Credit score continued to increase to 630 (Fair Isaac Corporation, 2025)[14].

Now that the credit scores meet the minimum FICO score requirement, we must work on establishing a budget, eliminating unnecessary expenses, and managing their money. The goal was to improve their financial situation further and create accessible cash flow by reducing expenses and preparing for a mortgage payment that would be significantly higher than what they were paying in rent.

I noticed that 10% of Mr. Taylor's income went to a 401(k) retirement plan. However, due to the immediate need to increase cash flow, I recommended that he temporarily suspend his participation in his 401k plan until he paid off all of his debt and established an emergency fund (Federal Reserve, 2024)[1]. Here's the reason why:

- He is not financially able to participate in a savings plan because he has no emergency fund.
- He has debt and no budget, so he spends money indiscriminately and doesn't know where his money is going.
- He has not saved any money for a down payment or closing costs.

Everybody's situation is different, so you may need to consult a Certified Financial Planner (CFP) if unsure what to do with your 401k. However, in Mr. Taylor's case, consulting a Certified Financial Planner (CFP) was not necessary to understand the basics of financial planning, which is to eliminate debt and establish a budget to save money; until you do those two essential things, you can save time and money on talking to CFPs.

So, we created a budget using mint.com. We could identify the unnecessary money he was spending on eating out, subscriptions, memberships, and other miscellaneous things. We found hundreds of dollars per month that could be saved. We agreed upon an amount that they could save monthly towards a down payment, closing costs, and an emergency fund. They decided not to restart his 401(k) plan, use their credit cards and carry a balance, finance any vehicles, or start any membership until they had achieved our goals for the down payment, closing cost, and emergency fund. They also agreed to eat out only once a month and start preparing meals at home and for lunch.

The plan had five main elements:

1. Paying off all debts.
2. Reducing expenses on luxuries and eating out
3. Reducing food and household expenses by buying in bulk.
4. Paying off balances immediately when they use their credit cards.
5. Creating an emergency fund and saving money for the down payment and closing costs (Federal Reserve, 2024)[1].

After six months, the Taylors had saved over 6k and had zero debt. Their credit scores were over 640 each, and Mr. Taylor canceled his 401(k). He decided to pay the penalty and use the money towards the down payment and closing costs. The penalty he paid was worth the future appreciation he would gain in homeownership by using the money for his down payment and closing costs.

In summary, after seven months of work and planning, Mr. And Ms. Taylor succeeded in the following:

- Improving their credit using a budget, saving secured credit. cards, and committing to changing their spending habits (Consumer Financial Protection Bureau, 2023)[7].
- Creating an emergency fund that eliminated their dependency on credit cards (Federal Reserve, 2024)[1].
- Obtaining a home with excellent terms and down payment assistance (U.S. Department of Housing and Urban Development, 2025)[55].

It took time, but we got it done because they were patient and willing to do the work. They did not use a credit repair agency. They did not do anything special. All they did was follow a plan. You can do it too.

CASE STUDY #2

Client: Bradley Simmons

Issue: Charge-offs

Bradley Simmons was referred to me because he was finally going to buy his first investment property—a duplex he planned to live in while renting out the other half. He had been putting it off for years while dealing with a job loss and the subsequent financial struggles.

Now, there was no stopping him. For one, he needed a change of environment; Bradley wanted to move into a quieter place in town. He also wanted to own the next home he moved into.

But there was a problem getting in the way of it all. Bradley had two charge-offs from two years before when he was unemployed and searching for a job. He could barely get by with his part-time hours within those two years; as a result, he could not make payments, and his credit score took a dive (Fair Isaac Corporation, 2025)[14].

"Charge-offs" can happen when you fail to pay your bills for months—usually six months in a row (Federal Trade Commission, 2023)[45]. After months of nonpayment, a creditor will eventually write off the debt as a loss in their records and cancel the account. However, the debtor is not on the hook; they are still responsible for paying back the debt. The charge can remain in your records for seven years, starting when your first missed payment is recorded (Federal Trade Commission, 2023)[45].

Bradley had now obtained a job, made decent money, and was back on his feet again. However, I advised him to get a better-paying job to settle with his creditors and pay off all his debt. He was not—in a position to buy now, given his chargeoffs and other debts. Within a few months, he could get a new job that paid better, and I advised him on how to start the settlement process.

Settling with your creditors is pretty straightforward. It just begins with communication (Consumer Financial Protection Bureau, 2023)[7]. You tell them about your circumstances, where you are now, and what you can do. They will make an offer, and then you will counter, and then they will make another offer, and then you will counter again. Do not expect the settlement process to happen in one meeting. It may take several sessions before you can come to a settlement. Do not be in a hurry to settle. The damage is done. Play the game because it is a game. If the creditor senses a real need for something to happen now, they will use that as leverage, not to negotiate a reduced settlement. So take your time.

It would help if you worked on your credit while the negotiation was going on to improve your score. I advised Bradley to obtain a new secured credit card of $1,000.00 (Consumer Financial Protection Bureau, 2023)[7]. This was all he could do then, but you can have a secure credit account for as little as 300 dollars or any amount you can afford. The larger the deposit, the larger the credit line, and the better it is for you and building credit.

Regardless of the credit limit, Bradley understood that he had to keep his credit utilization under 30% (Fair Isaac Corporation, 2025)[14]. To ensure he never approached the limit, I advised him only to charge what he could pay off at the end of each month. We established a credit restoration plan, a debt elimination plan, a savings plan, and a budget to eliminate unnecessary expenses (Bankrate, 2025)[27]. After six months, Bradley was able to achieve the following results:

- Bradley cleared the charge-offs from his credit report by settling with his creditors (Federal Trade Commission, 2023)[45]. He also opened additional secured credit cards to build his credit further (Consumer Financial Protection Bureau, 2023)[7].
- With the new, secured credit cards, he raised his score significantly and could now meet the minimum FICO score requirement for the mortgage loan (Fair Isaac Corporation, 2025)[14].
- Bradley eliminated going out to eat, subscriptions to various computer programs, and even his gym membership. But, of course, he never went to the gym anyway. Just budgeting alone saved him over $1000 a month. Bradley also saved two months of his income for an emergency fund and additional money with part-time jobs for the down payment and closing costs (Federal Reserve, 2024)[1].

- Bradley was also able to qualify for a mortgage to purchase a duplex in the quieter area of the town because he had no debt, and the bank could use the rent from the other unit to help him qualify (Bankrate, 2025)[27].
- Best of all, he could qualify for down payment assistance, allowing him to retain his reserves after purchasing the home (U.S. Department of Housing and Urban Development, 2025)[55].

Today, Bradley lives in his dream home and continues to take steps to keep his credit record clean and his credit score high (Fair Isaac Corporation, 2025)[14]. He can also pay part of his mortgage with passive income from the rented space and is saving even more money to build his emergency fund to 6 months of his monthly take-home pay. All home buyers should consider purchasing a 2 to 4-unit property to establish the permanency that homeownership brings, increase their income, and make meeting the new mortgage obligation much easier.

CASE STUDY #3

Client: Mr. and Mrs. Vaughn

Issue: Low credit score, high debt-to-income ratio

Mr. and Mrs. Vaughn, a California couple living in Fresno with three teenage children, decided to buy a new home for their twentieth anniversary. They had lived in their first apartment since getting married.

While they had enjoyed living in the house over the years, their first daughter Karen had to leave for college in Los Angeles, and they were considering moving there to be closer to her. Additionally, Mrs. Vaughn's brother, Darren, was relocating to Fresno with his young family. Letting Darren's family stay with them for a few months was a no-brainer because they were family, but they needed space.

Mrs. Vaughn was referred to me by her coworker Anne, a former client. The couple was excited about buying their first home, and I was equally excited for them. Life was changing, and they needed room. Unfortunately, Mrs. Vaughn's FICO was 500, and Mr. Vaughn's was

560. Combined with their high debt-to-income ratio, they would not be able to qualify for a loan (Fair Isaac Corporation, 2025)[14]. The excitement turned to disappointment because they had no idea that their credit scores were so low and their debt-to-income ratios were so high. Their scores were low because they paid late every month on everything. Also, their debt-to-income ratio was high because they were both leasing cars (Bankrate, 2025)[27]. The two-car payments totaled $1,200 a month. How do you buy a home or save money by paying out 1,200 dollars a month in car payments? You do not.

FHA will allow credit scores as low as 580, but most banks have a minimum score of 620 (MyFICO, 2025)[26]. Mr. Vaughn's was closest to the mark. I advised them to pay off their credit card debt, sell their cars, and establish a budget using mint.com. I know what you are thinking. Sell the car? How are they going to get to work? The answer is that they would have to buy another car or use a family member's car that was not being used until they could afford to pay cash for a vehicle or put a down payment on more affordable used cars. So after being in shock for a few minutes from the advice I gave them, they decided that tough love was what they needed. They knew the day they bought the cars that it was a wrong financial decision, and they have been struggling to keep up with their living expenses.

So here's what they did:

They immediately put both cars for sale on auto trader. In both cases, the offers came in below what they owed on the vehicles. They were able to get help from their parents to make up the difference to pay off the cars so that they could sell them. On one car, they needed $5000, and on the other vehicle, they needed $3000. I would've preferred that the $8000 would've been used as a gift towards the down payment on their new home, but they needed to get rid of $1200 a month in debt.

In addition, their parents and one of his uncles had extra vehicles just sitting in the yard. One needed some mechanical work that cost about $300; the other just needed gas. So they were fortunate to have family members with cars they were not using to replace the vehicles they were making payments on.

We established a budget using mint.com, identified unnecessary expenses, memberships, and subscriptions, and canceled everything. They were spending $400 a month on dog grooming and dog food. They saved almost $400 a month just by eating out on the weekends and during the week. In addition to buying groceries in bulk and making all the changes in their budget, they could save almost $2000 a month.

In addition, they were both involved side online businesses and multilevel businesses. So they decided to step up their game to generate more income from those businesses to create more income for the household. This was a significant move because even though we had found additional money, it still wasn't enough.

We still needed to pay off credit card debt, establish an emergency fund, and save money for a new home's down payment and closing costs (Federal Reserve, 2024)[1]. So we set up a credit restoration plan and established additional trade lines with secured credit cards (Consumer Financial Protection Bureau, 2023)[7]. We set an emergency fund plan, a debt elimination plan, and a savings plan for the down payment. Hence, the extra money coming in and the savings we found in creating a budget.

After twelve months of applying the recommended strategies:

Mr. Vaughn's credit score went from 560 to 680, an increase of 120 points (Fair Isaac Corporation, 2025)[14]. How? Three one thousand dollar secured credit cards that carried no balances (Consumer Financial Protection Bureau, 2023)[7]. Mrs. Vaughn's score also increased from 500 to 640. How? Three secured credit cards Ranging from 500 to 2000. She never carried a balance. The credit cards are paid off every single month (Fair Isaac Corporation, 2025)[14].

They also saved $10,000 and were able to qualify for a conventional loan with down payment assistance (U.S. Department of Housing and Urban Development, 2025)[55]. The couple obtained their dream home in Los Angeles right before their anniversary. Their life has changed. They have no debt. They have excellent credit. They have continued to build their emergency fund and are living on a budget and saving money (Federal Reserve, 2024)[1]. They are committed to building their emergency fund for 12 months as their income before they take on any new financial obligations. Cash is king in their home.

CASE STUDY #4

Client: Claire Stewart

Issue: Low FICO Score: 600

Claire Stewart came to me wanting to qualify for a home loan with down payment assistance. Her credit score was 600 (Fair Isaac Corporation, 2025)[14]. She has less than three thousand dollars in the bank and a high income of 90,000 yearly. Based on your income and the fact that it's just her, she should have much more money in the bank. Instead, she was in debt of $25,000 in credit card debt, and her monthly payments barely covered the interest. She also had a luxury car with a balance of 80k and monthly payments of$1200.

On a positive note, she contributed 10% of her income to her 401(k) and accumulated $60,000 in the last six years. She was currently saving some money in taxes, but she was also dealing with limited cash flow after taxes, rent, food, utilities, credit card, and auto payment. Her rent alone was almost $2500 a month.

You should know the first thing I told her to do by now. Get rid of the car. No one should be spending that much money on a vehicle. I mean, if you are that rich, pay cash. Why would you pay interest and fees for anything if you had the money? Interest is extra. Don't let anyone fool you; leasing and financing cars are for poor people who don't have any money. The expensive vehicles they pulled up to their rented apartment or house prove they are broke. Let's be clear on this. Nobody pays interest unless they have to. The only exception would be on a home. Buy a house first and then buy a car. If you must finance it because you don't have the cash to pay for it, then at least buy a house first.

In addition, the car payment was high because her credit score was low. The lower the credit score, the higher the interest rate (Fair Isaac Corporation, 2025)[14].

Secondly, to pay off the credit card debt and establish a budget using mint.com. She is making so much money that she doesn't balance her bank account, check her credit score, think about saving money, or plan for the future. All she wanted to do was buy a house with down payment assistance because she had no money saved and no clue what she was about to get into. Buying a home is more than just making payments. And if you are renting an apartment, then you have no idea about the additional cost associated with maintenance and keeping up the property. How she lived, and her lifestyle showed that she was not ready yet to become a homeowner. So we had to go to work and get ready for homeownership. So here is what she did:

She listed the car on Auto Trader. It got an offer, but it was for 10,000 less than what she owed on the vehicle. So she couldn't sell the car because she had no money. We had to develop a plan to acquire the 10,000 so that she could pay for the car when she put it back on the market again, and we needed to do it quickly. Keeping the vehicle was not an option. So, the fastest solution was to get a loan against her 401(k) so she would have the money to make up the difference. She put the car back on the market, sold it within a couple of weeks, and got rid of the debt and car payment. $1200 a month! She then went and paid cash for a used car. She borrowed $20,000 from her 401(k) to sell the car and buy a used car. She paid $8000 for a newer used Toyota.

With the car gone and $1200 a month in extra cash flow, we started working on the budget (Bankrate, 2025)[27]. We established a budget and eliminated many unnecessary expenses. She agreed to stop eating out daily, bring her meals to work, and start cooking at home. She agreed to eliminate her cable bill of $300 a month. She rarely watches TV anyway, so she's signed up for Hulu and Netflix.

We establish a debt elimination plan, a savings plan for the down payment and closing cost, and an emergency fund (Federal Reserve, 2024)[1]. After all was said and done, she saved almost $3000 a month. That's a lot of money.

This additional money made the credit restoration plan very easy. She established three $1000 savings-secured visa cards immediately (Consumer Financial Protection Bureau, 2023)[7]. She paid off her existing credit cards because many had late payments, but she did not close those accounts. She continued using the cards but paid out the balances every month.

After six months of applying the recommended strategies:

Claire's credit score rose 100 points to 700 (Fair Isaac Corporation, 2025)[14]. How? She kept zero balances on her credit cards and added two more secured Visa cards with a limit of 2000 each (Consumer Financial Protection Bureau, 2023)[7]. She also maintains a capacity ratio of 100% by paying the balance owed on time every month (Fair Isaac Corporation, 2025)[14].

Claire paid off her overall debt in full. However, having no debt laid the foundation for saving more money. She built her emergency fund by eliminating unnecessary expenses and living on a budget (Federal Reserve, 2024)[1]. Between her savings accounts with secured visas and her regular savings account, she saved close to $20,000 in her emergency fund.

Claire Decided to close her 401(k) account. The money she borrowed was then reduced from her 401k account, and she no longer had payment deductions from her paycheck. She then uses the balance after penalties for withdrawal and taxes for the down payment on a brand-new home (U.S. Department of Housing and Urban Development, 2025)[55].

Claire got serious about becoming financially literate. She never really sat down until she decided to buy a house to look at how she was spending money and that she had no real goals or plans. Claire didn't take credit seriously, nor did she take saving money seriously, nor did she fully understand the 401k. She thought that if she had a 401(k), she would be fine. A 401(k) is not an emergency fund. It is a long-term retirement fund.

You should establish an emergency fund first, invest in the market second to save money to buy a home, and before you start investing in a long-term saving program (Federal Reserve, 2024)[1]. You should not participate in a retirement fund because you should not invest in the market until you establish an emergency fund. It's just that simple.

CASE STUDY CONCLUSION

In all four case studies, it took six months to a year to get these families back on track. You didn't get into debt overnight, and you're not going to get out of it overnight. It took years of financial abuse and mismanagement that led to their financial crisis and inability to purchase a home (Consumer Financial Protection Bureau, 2023)[7]. In all four cases, when they were finally ready to buy a home, they ended up paying more for the house had they been prepared to buy the home when they first began the process. In all four cases, had they been ready to buy a home when they initially started, they would've saved money in the payment and interest they were paying (Bankrate, 2025)[27]. Procrastinating costs them money. Bad credit, not having savings, and not being prepared to buy a home then cost them more money.

Unfortunately, many people have failed to address the issues with their credit by saving money and getting themselves in a position to buy. They have waited too long, and the market has simply left them behind. The prices of homes are skyrocketing, and interest rates continue to rise (Federal Reserve Bank of New York, 2023)[9]. For many, they have been priced out completely and may have to move. If you're priced out, don't give up. Instead, consider partnering up with a family member or friend and joining forces to buy a multiple-unit property or even a single-family home.

Homeownership is not just an aspiration goal that you should do, and it is now a matter of survival. The cost of housing and the cost of living will continue to rise (Federal Reserve, 2024)[1]. You need to have a place you can call your own when you retire. All of us are going to get old. There will come a time when you will not be able to work or earn the money that rent will require. You must buy a home now and work to pay it off as soon as possible. Your Power Is Now!

DID YOU ENJOY THIS BOOK?

I sure hope so!

Please join our family and write a review. Reviews are the "tip jar" of the book publishing industry. New readers weigh reviews heavily in deciding to make a purchase. You being so generous as to share your experience is the lifeblood of the success of "The Credit Handbook" To do this please scan the QR code below

I appreciate you!
Eric Lawrence Frazier

BECOME A MEMBER TODAY

Why Become a Member of The Power Is Now Media?

Unlock exclusive access to the most powerful real estate, mortgage, credit, and wealth-building content in the industry.

For a limited time, become a member for only $10/month or $60/year. Your membership delivers undeniable value, insider access, and proven tools to help you buy, sell, invest, and build wealth with confidence.

Membership Benefits

Exclusive Streaming & Shows

- Unlimited access to The Power Is Now TV Network library of hundreds of shows, podcasts, and webinars.
- Daily programming on homeownership, real estate investing, mortgages, credit, and financial literacy (Federal Reserve, 2024)[1].

- Member-only live streams and roundtable discussions with top industry leaders.

Free Digital Resources

- Real estate eBooks, guides, and reports on buying, selling, investing, and credit strategies (Consumer Financial Protection Bureau, 2023)[7].
- Buyer & Seller Guides, HUD Homes Guide, and Foreclosure Market Reports, updated quarterly (U.S. Department of Housing and Urban Development, 2025)[55].
- Access to The Power Is Now Media Resource Library of downloadable content.

Magazines & Newsletters

- Complimentary subscription to The Power Is Now National Real Estate Magazine.
- Complimentary subscription to The Power Is Now HUD Homes for Sale Magazine.
- Complimentary subscription to The Power Is Now TV Guide Magazine.
- Complimentary subscription to Faith, Family & Finance Magazine.
- Weekly newsletters with videos, infographics, and market insights (Federal Reserve Bank of New York, 2023)[9].

Member Engagement

- Invitations to attend and participate in live recordings of the Real Estate Roundtable and Business Roundtable.
- Networking opportunities with agents, lenders, investors, and entrepreneurs nationwide.
- Priority access to quarterly webinars for first-time

homebuyers, investors, and asset managers (U.S. Department of Housing and Urban Development, 2025)[55].

- Monthly group coaching sessions on Personal Finance, Real Estate, Mortgage, and Media (Federal Reserve, 2024)[1].

Discounts & Savings

- Member-only discounts on media services (podcast hosting, YouTube TV production, private-label magazines, website redesigns, social media management).
- Exclusive pricing on advertising, sponsorships, and coaching programs.

Community & Recognition

- Become part of a national network of professionals and consumers committed to real estate wealth-building.
- Opportunities to feature your story, listings, or business on The Power Is Now TV Network.

SPECIAL MEMBERSHIP OFFER

Join now at www.thepowerisnow.com

Special Launch Price: $10/month or $60/year (limited-time offer through year-end).

Regular Price: $50/month or $325/year.

Don't wait—membership pays for itself many times over.

For over 16 years, The Power Is Now has been dedicated to educating and empowering people in real estate, mortgage, credit, and wealth-building (Consumer Financial Protection Bureau, 2023)[7]. Now, through our membership program, you can unlock exclusive access to everything we offer.

For only $10 a month or $60 a year, you'll get unlimited access to hundreds of shows on The Power Is Now TV Network, free eBooks and real estate guides, four magazine subscriptions, weekly newsletters, and live roundtable access with industry leaders. You'll also enjoy discounts on media services, group coaching, and the chance to network with professionals across the country.

But here's the best part—you'll be part of a movement. A national community committed to real estate wealth-building, financial literacy, and creating generational wealth (Federal Reserve, 2024)[1].

So go to www.thepowerisnow.com today and become a member. This special pricing is only available until the end of the year. Join us, and let's build wealth together.

SCAN ME

ABOUT THE AUTHOR

Mr. Eric Lawrence Frazier, MBA, is the President and CEO of The Power Is Now Media, a national multimedia company dedicated to real estate education, empowerment, and thought leadership. Through its expansive platform—comprising the Power Is Now website (www.thepowerisnow.com), national podcast networks, social media channels, and live-stream television platforms—the company delivers timely, authoritative content on real estate, lending, economics, and government policy.

In addition to leading the media network, Mr. Frazier serves as the Publisher and Editor-in-Chief of The Power Is Now Publishing, which produces books and magazines dedicated to real estate, financial literacy, and wealth building (Federal Reserve, 2024)[1]. Since its founding, the publishing division has created a wide range of educational materials, including **The Power Is Now Magazines**, a suite of online real estate publications launched in 2013 that feature market insights, national news, and educational resources for both homebuyers and professionals.

Mr. Frazier is a graduate of the University of Redlands in Redlands, California, where he earned a Master of Business Administration (MBA) with an emphasis in Finance as well as a Bachelor of Science in Business Administration and Management. He has lectured on the U.S. mortgage crisis at the University of California, Riverside, addressing international business leaders from India, and has served as an adjunct professor.

With nearly four decades of expertise in mortgage banking, Mr. Frazier is nationally recognized for his leadership in origination, underwriting, operations, management, and marketing (Federal Reserve Bank of New York, 2023)[9]. He has also built a distinguished career in real estate sales and brokerage, holding a California real estate license for over thirty years and a broker's license (#01143484) for more than twenty-eight years. Together with his wife, he founded Frazier Group Realty (www.fraziergrouprealty.com), a full-service, family-owned real estate company based in Riverside, California.

Mr. Frazier's professional leadership extends into numerous industry associations. He is the former President of the Orange County Realtist chapter of the National Association of Real Estate Brokers (NAREB) and a former Director of the California Association of Real Estate Brokers. He has also served as Vice President of the Orange County chapter of the National Association of Hispanic Real Estate Professionals (NAHREP) and as an Advisory Board Member of the Orange County chapter of the Asian Real Estate Association of America (AREAA). He has served on the Board of Directors of the Riverside Fair Housing Council, was a past member of the Pacific West Association of Realtors, and is currently a member of the Inland Valley Association of Realtors (IVAR).

Beyond real estate, Mr. Frazier is deeply engaged in civic and community leadership. He has served on the Board of Directors of Project Tomorrow (www.tomorrow.org), a national nonprofit organization dedicated to education. He is an active member of the 100 Black Men of America, the NAACP, and the National Association of Mortgage Brokers. He is also the past President and Director of the State of California African American Museum (www.caamuseum.org).

His spiritual leadership is rooted in the church. Mr. Frazier is a pastor and leads The Power Is Now Ministries, a ministry of the North Fontana Church, a 501(c)(non-profit) organization, where he continues to serve through teaching, outreach, and mentorship.

A man of diverse talents, Mr. Frazier is also an author, blogger, poet, singer, songwriter, motivational speaker, business consultant, and coach to both for-profit and nonprofit organizations, as well as a personal financial coach (Federal Reserve, 2024)[1]. He is the published author of six books spanning poetry, African American wealth, credit, and business. His personal interests include golf, running, and jazz music.

Mr. Frazier is especially committed to mentorship, striving to be a role model for African American men and dedicating time to coaching young people and adults. His greatest joy, however, is found in family. He has been married to the love of his life, Ruby, for over forty years, and together they have raised four accomplished daughters. His three eldest daughters hold master's degrees in management and business, while his youngest has earned a bachelor's degree in apparel merchandising and management.

All of Mr. Frazier's professional accomplishments, affiliations, and ongoing work can be found at www.linkedin.com/in/ericfrazier.

FOLLOW ME ON SOCIAL MEDIA
LET'S CONNECT ON LINKEDIN

- facebook.com/thepowerisnow
- x.com/thepowerisnow
- instagram.com/thepowerisnow
- linkedin.com/company/thepowerisnow
- pinterest.com/thepowerisnow1
- amazon.com/stores/Eric-Lawrence-Frazier/author/B07S6CFKWN?ref=ap_rdr&isDramIntegrated=true&shoppingPortalEnabled=true

ABOUT THE POWER IS NOW MEDIA

The Power Is Now Media is an online multimedia company founded in 2009 by Eric L. Frazier MBA, headquartered in Riverside, California. We are advocates for homeownership, wealth building, and financial literacy (Federal Reserve, 2024)[1]. We create and publish original educational content about real estate through nationally syndicated Radio, Podcasts, Magazines, TV, Social Media, Streaming platforms, and special online seminars and webinars.

We are an online platform and resource for everyone to learn about homeownership, housing, loan programs, and down payment assistance to achieve financial literacy and the American dream of homeownership (U.S. Department of Housing and Urban Development, 2025)[55]. We are supported by housing finance agencies, real estate associations, and civic, religious, and community organizations. We help them amplify their voice about the services and programs they offer in lending, housing, and homeownership. Visit us at www.thepowerisnow.com

The Mission of the Power is Now Media is to inspire and educate consumers and real estate professionals to build wealth through the acquisition, management, and sale of real estate with information and support we provide via our website, live and on-demand TV, and social media platforms that empower everyone to own real estate now and achieve the American dream of homeownership (Consumer Financial Protection Bureau, 2023)[7]. Our company slogan is "We are leading the conversation about real homeownership."

The Power Is Now Media corporate office is located at 3739 6th Street, Riverside, CA 92501. Telephone/Fax: 800-401-8994. Eric Lawrence Frazier MBA is a California Licensed Loan Originator (NMLS License #461807) and Real Estate Broker (License #O1148434).

REFERENCES

[1] Federal Reserve. *Consumer Credit – G.19 Report.* Board of Governors of the Federal Reserve System, 2024.

[2] U.S. Department of Education. *Federal Student Loan Portfolio,* 2024.

[3] Gramm-Leach-Bliley Act, 15 U.S.C. § 6801–6809 (1999).

[4] MarketScreener.com. "Fair Isaac Corp. Company Profile," 2025.

[5] Barron's. "FICO's Market Power." May 2025.

[6] Cato Institute. "Algorithmic Accountability in Credit Scoring," 2024.

[7] Consumer Financial Protection Bureau (CFPB). *Your Credit Score.* Washington, DC, 2023.

[8] Federal Reserve. *Economic Well-Being of U.S. Households in 2020.* Washington, DC, 2021.

[9] Federal Reserve Bank of New York. *Quarterly Report on Household Debt and Credit.* New York, NY, 2023.

[10] Government Accountability Office (GAO). *Credit Reporting Agencies: Market Structure and Consumer Impact.* Washington, DC, 2022.

[11] U.S. Department of Justice (DOJ). *Combatting Redlining Initiative: Case Summaries.* Washington, DC, 2023.

[12] U.S. Securities and Exchange Commission (SEC). *Fair Isaac Corporation Annual Report.* Washington, DC, 2023.

[13] World Bank. *Global Experiences with Credit Reporting and Alternative Data.* Washington, DC, 2021.

[14] Fair Isaac Corporation. *Definitive Proxy Statement (DEF 14A),* filed January 27, 2025.

[15] Fair Isaac Corporation. *Beneficial Ownership Table (2025 Proxy Excerpt).* U.S. Securities and Exchange Commission.

[16] MarketScreener. *Fair Isaac Corporation—Proxy/Board Nominees Extract (hosted).* Accessed Aug. 2025.

[17] Barron's. "FICO Stock's Premium Valuation Reflects Its Scoring Grip." Accessed Aug. 2025.

[18] Politico. "Justice Dept. Opens Antitrust Probe Into Credit-Scoring Giant." July 2020.

[19] Reuters. "FICO Loses Bid to Dismiss Antitrust Claims Over Credit-Scoring Market." Sept. 2023.

[20] Federal Trade Commission. *Gramm-Leach-Bliley Act (GLBA) Privacy Rule Guidance.* https://www.ftc.gov/business-guidance/privacy-security/gramm-leach-bliley-act

[21] Consumer Financial Protection Bureau. *Market Snapshot: Credit Reporting (overview pages and reports).* https://www.consumerfinance.gov/

[22] Congressional Research Service. *The Glass-Steagall Act: A Legal and Policy Analysis (R44349).* Jan. 19, 2016. https://www.congress.gov/crs-product/R44349

[23] Federal Deposit Insurance Corporation (FDIC). *History of the 1930s Banking Reforms (Glass-Steagall context).* https://www.fdic.gov/history/1930-1939

[24] The Balance. https://www.thebalance.com/

[25] TransUnion. https://www.transunion.com/

[26] myFICO. https://www.myfico.com/

[27] Bankrate. https://www.bankrate.com/

[28] NerdWallet. https://www.nerdwallet.com/

[29] Investopedia. https://www.investopedia.com/

[30] Credit Karma. https://www.creditkarma.com/

[31] Credit Card Insider. https://www.creditcardinsider.com/blog/highest-credit-score/

[32] Time Money. http://time.com/money/collection-post/2791957/what-is-my-credit-score/

[33] Dough Roller. https://www.doughroller.net/credit/how-to-track-all-3-credit-scores/

[34] BlueWater Credit. https://bluewatercredit.com/FICO-Score-8-vs-Other-Versions

[35] APR Finder. https://www.aprfinder.com/how-many-fico-credit-score-versions-models

[36] Valiant Credit. https://www.valiantcredit.com/blog/49-fico-score-models

[37] NerdWallet (FICO Score 9). https://www.nerdwallet.com/blog/finance/fico-score-9/

[38] MyFICO (Education Page). https://www.myfico.com/credit-education/credit-scores/fico-score-versions

[39] Federal Aviation Administration (FAA). *Credit Score Fact Sheet,* March 2023.

[40] MyFICO Blog. https://blog.myfico.com/fico-score-9-whats-the-difference/

[41] MyFICO Identity Theft Education. https://www.myfico.com/credit-education/identity-theft

[42] America Saves. https://americasaves.org/for-savers/debt-and-credit/importance-of-credit-history

[43] Investopedia (Credit Worthiness). https://www.investopedia.com/terms/c/credit-worthiness.asp

[44] Experian (Ask Experian). https://www.experian.com/blogs/ask-experian/credit-education/score-basics/what-is-a-good-credit-score/

[45] Federal Trade Commission. *Fair Credit Reporting Act.* https://www.ftc.gov/system/files/545a_fair-credit-reporting-act.pdf

[46] Consumer Affairs. https://www.consumeraffairs.com/finance/how-to-build-credit.html

[47] USA Today. https://www.usatoday.com/story/money/personal finance/2017/02/06/identity-theft-hit-all-time-high-2016/97398548/

[48] Consumer Reports. https://www.consumerreports.org/cro/2010/07/protect-your-identity/index.htm

[49] TransUnion Article. https://www.transunion.com/article/before-creating-a-password-use-this-checklist

[50] The Balance (FCRA). https://www.thebalance.com/what-you-should-know-about-the-fcra-960639

[51] Annual Credit Report. https://www.annualcreditreport.com/

[52] Bankrate (Mortgage Rate). https://www.bankrate.com/finance/mortgages/how-credit-scores-impact-your-mortgage-rate-1.aspx

Made in the USA
Coppell, TX
20 March 2026

74174262R00090